Witchcraft

B-24 LIBERATOR

WARBIRD FLIGHTLINE 001

KENNY KEMP

WITCHCRAFT: B-24 LIBERATOR
Copyright © 2017 Kemp Enterprises, Inc.

Book Design: Kenny Kemp · Photographic Consultant: Douglas Page
Front Cover Illustration: Ron Cole · Back Cover Photo: James Preve
Copyrighted photos are labeled. Unlabeled photos are believed to be in the public domain.

Library of Congress Cataloging-in-Publication Data

Names: Kemp, Kenny, author.
Title: Witchcraft : B-24 Liberator / by Kenny Kemp.
Other titles: B-24 Liberator
Description: First edition.
Salt Lake City : Alta Films Press, an imprint of Kemp Enterprises, Inc., [2017]
Series: Warbird flightline ; 001
Includes bibliographical references.
Identifiers: LCCN 2017008498 | ISBN 9781892442758 (oversize pbk. : alk. paper)
Subjects: LCSH: World War, 1939-1945--Aerial operations, American.
Witchcraft (B-24 bomber) | B-24 (Bomber)--History. | World War, 1939-1945--Campaigns.
Classification: LCC D790 .K435 2017 | DDC 940.54/4973--dc23
LC record available at https://lccn.loc.gov/2017008498

First Printing

Alta Films
P R E S S

Published by Alta Films Press, an imprint of Kemp Enterprises, Inc.
Printed in South Korea by Four Colour Print Group, Louisville, KY.

www.kennykemp.com
www.witchcraftb24.com

FOREWORD

If you were to enter my office and see a baseball sitting on my desk among the papers and books, you might think it out of place. Or maybe its a "ponder prop"—something a writer holds and perhaps kneads as he's thinking over an idea.

You might consider its construction: a cork center, wound with a mile of yarn and covered with two figure-8 shaped strips of white horsehide stitched tightly together with red thread.

Or perhaps you know that I'm a pilot and a baseball's stitches act like airfoils, catching the wind and causing the ball to swerve on its trajectory, making pitching a baseball almost as interesting as instrument flight.

Looking closer, you might note that it's scuffed and a little dirty. Just a baseball.

But what if I told you that baseball—the very one you're holding in your hand—was the first pitch thrown by relief pitcher Barney Schultz late in Game 3 of the 1964 World Series between the New York Yankees and the St. Louis Cardinals, and that Mickey Mantle, batting right-handed that day, blasted that very baseball into the right field stands at Yankee Stadium, winning the game for the Yankees, 2-1. And more: that homer, Mantle's 16th World Series round-tripper, broke the record of 15 set by none other than Mickey's fellow Yankee, Babe Ruth.

You gingerly place the ball on the desk and whistle low. Wow. That's *some* baseball.

Context is everything. A baseball is just a baseball until you know its trajectory, so to speak. And an airplane is just an airplane until you know why it flew. That's why I've spent the first portion of the book you're holding telling you why the world desperately needed the B-24 Liberator and how it arrived at the right time; how it fought in every theater of the war; how it went from concept to prototype in just nine months; how they built more of them than any military aircraft in American history; how, by the end of the war, it was already obsolete and destined for the boneyard; and how it saved my father's life, and by extension, mine as well.

Or maybe it's just an airplane the way that baseball is just a baseball.

Don't you believe it.

– Kenny Kemp

DEDICATION

To the boys who became men... and then became heroes.

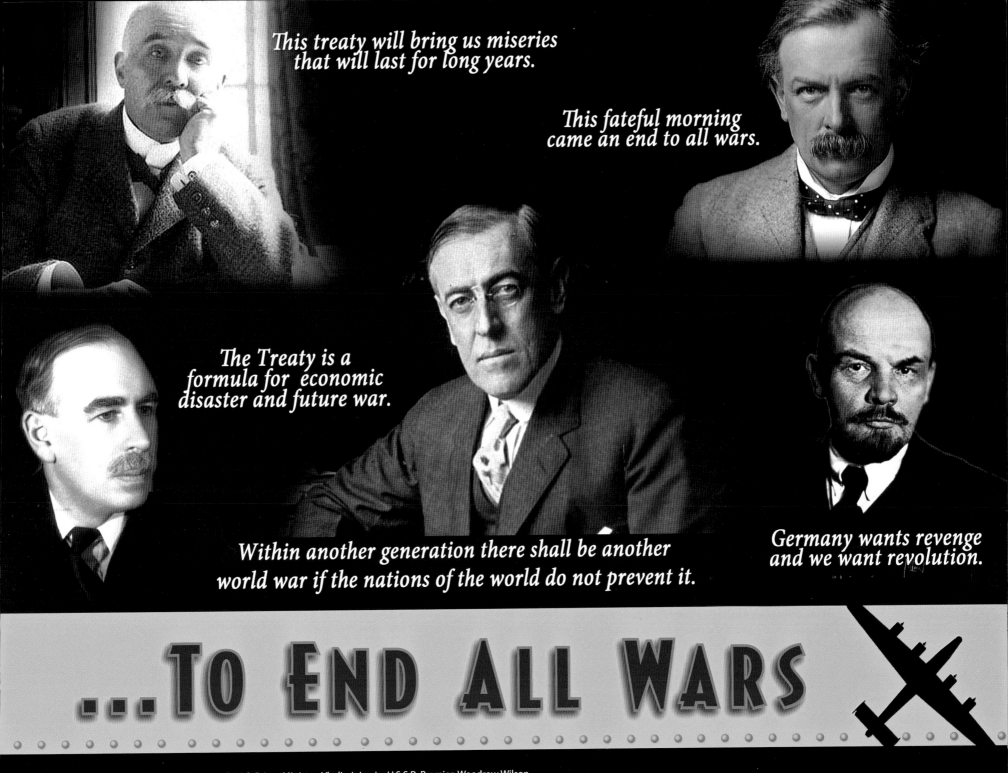

This treaty will bring us miseries that will last for long years.

This fateful morning came an end to all wars.

The Treaty is a formula for economic disaster and future war.

Within another generation there shall be another world war if the nations of the world do not prevent it.

Germany wants revenge and we want revolution.

...TO END ALL WARS

Clockwise from upper right: Lloyd George, British Prime Minister; Vladimir Lenin, U.S.S.R. Premier; Woodrow Wilson, American President; John Maynard Keynes, British economist; Georges Clemenceau, French Prime Minister

CONFLICTS ARISE

FOR CENTURIES, Europe was ruled by monarchies forged by the Catholic Church, families, and marriage, uniting disparate peoples and races. The catalyst of World War I occurred in 1890 when Germany's Kaiser Wilhelm II refused to renew a treaty with Russia. In response, France allied with Russia, as did the United Kingdom, creating the Triple Entente. Wilhelm, challenging the U.K.'s dominance of the seas, ramped up Germany's military spending and Europe responded in kind. In 1908, the Austro-Hungarian Empire formally annexed Bosnia and Herzogovina, which were part of the Ottoman Empire, but which the Austro-Hungarians had occupied for over thirty years.

In June 1914, during a visit to Bosnia, Austro-Hungarian heir Archduke Franz Ferdinand was assassinated by Serbian radicals in Sarajevo, which led to his Empire's declaration of war against Serbia, whose ally Russia mobilized in defense. In support of Austria-Hungary, Germany also mobilized its army.

Wilhelm asked his cousin, Tsar Nicolas II of Russia, to suspend mobilization, but Nicolas refused. So, on 1 August 1914, Germany declared war on Russia and shortly thereafter invaded France to discourage its support for Russia.

The German advance was stopped in the Somme District north of Paris, where the Western Front bogged down in a battle of attrition and trench warfare where little changed for three long years as hundreds of thousands died on both sides.

Military alliances in 1914

- Central Powers
- Triple Entente
- Slavic allies of Russia
- → minority groups in Austria–Hungary

LEFT The pickelhaube ("spike bonnet") Prussian officer's helmet made of boiled (hardened) leather.

BACKGROUND Canadian soldiers cross no-man's land in the Battle of Vimy Ridge, near Nord-Pas-de-Calais, France, April 1917.

EMPIRES FALL

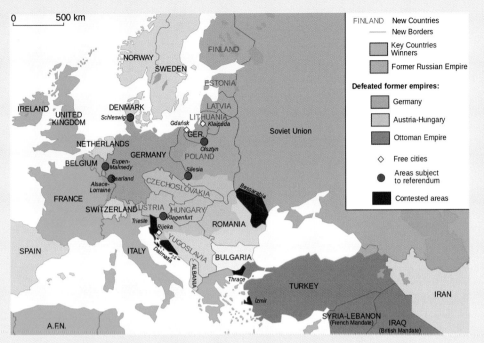

IN AUGUST 1914, pursuant to its treaty with Russia, the United Kingdom declared war on the Central Powers (Germany, Austria-Hungary, and Italy). Shortly thereafter, Russia invaded East Prussia. The Ottoman Empire, unrest already within its borders, joined the Central Powers and opened fronts against the Allies in the Middle East.

In 1915, Italy rethought its future and joined the Allies, and Bulgaria joined the Central Powers. The following year, Romania joined the Allies, as did the United States in 1917.

With America now in the war, the Central Powers began to feel the pinch, but in March 1917 they received an unexpected boon: The Russian tsarist government collapsed and by November a full-scale Bolshevik communist revolution resulted in the Treaty of Brest-Litovsk, which ended hostilities on the Eastern Front.

Accordingly, in the spring of 1918 Germany opened a major offensive on the Western Front. The Allies rallied and drove the Germans back in their 100 Day Offensive. In April, Austria-Hungary agreed to an armistice, and by November, Germany did the same.

By the end of the war, 37 million people had died and the dynasties which had ruled the German, Austro-Hungarian, Ottoman, and Russian Empires for generations had collapsed. National borders were redrawn, new independent nations were formed, and Germany's worldwide colonies were parceled out to the winners. And in 1919, at the peace conference in Paris, President Wilson's dream of a new world order under the auspices of a League of Nations was unveiled.

It would only make matters worse.

BACKGROUND British soldiers go "over the top" at the Somme, in northern France, in the worst day of fighting in World War I in which 60,000 British soldiers were killed.

RIGHT Belgian Army gas mask. There were an estimated 1.3 million casualties from gas attacks.

SALTING THE EARTH

GERMAN DIPLOMATS arrived in Paris in early 1919, unbowed. The Allies had never invaded the motherland and its army, millions strong, had retreated in good order while its enemies lay in ruin. It was hard for Germans to see how they had lost the war. President Woodrow Wilson, who brought America into the war to give it a voice in the peace process, promised General Ludendorff that Germany would not be dismembered. However, the French and British, who had lost millions of men, opposed many of Wilson's ideas and instead focused on rewards for the victors and punishment for the vanquished.

This meant disarmament, territory concession, and reparations. Article 231 (the "War Guilt Clause") codified the case: Germany must "acknowledge responsibility for all loss and damage to which the Allied and Associated Governments and their nationals have been subjected as a consequence of the war imposed upon them by German aggression."

German diplomats complained Germany was being singled out because of all the Central Powers, it had the only intact economy. President Wilson agreed, but allowed Georges Clemenceau of France and Lloyd George of the U.K. to outflank him, primarily because both France and England owed millions to the United States in war loan debt.

As the only Allied country to share a border with Germany, France demanded and obtained the demilitarization of the Rhineland buffer zone and control over the Saar, the site of Germany's coal industry. In addition, Germany was stripped of 25,000 square miles of territory and over 7 million people. It also lost colonies all over the world.

But what angered Germany most was that it was excluded from the peace negotiations. Calling the Treaty an "affront to honor "and a "murderous plan," the German delegation withdrew from the conference in disgust. But just hours before the signing deadline, the German National Assembly, knowing that the Allies were ready to invade Germany, reluctantly ratified the Treaty, though they called it a "stab in the back." British economist John Maynard Keynes termed it a "Carthaginian peace" and a misguided attempt to destroy Germany. But as far as the Allies were concerned, it was just desserts.

BACKGROUND Citizens and soldiers alike press forward toward the Palace of Versailles, where treaty negotiations are being announced, November 1918.

ABOVE The German delegation meets at Versailles.
MIDDLE Allied leaders, L-R: English Prime Minister David Lloyd, Italian Prime Minister Vittorio Orlando, French Prime Minister Georges Clemenceau, and U.S. President Woodrow Wilson.

A REVOLT BY German sailors just before the end of the war paved the way for a German revolution which resulted in it becoming a parliamentary republic. A coalition led by the leftist Social Democrat Party nevertheless abhorred the totalitarianism into which Russia had plunged. Strikes wracked the country and gave voice to bitterly competitive nationalist, socialist, and anti-democratic impulses.

Prior to WWI, Germany had dispensed with the gold standard, opting instead to finance the war by borrowing. This devalued the mark, which led to hyper-inflation after the war. Reparations recipients refused to accept marks, requiring payment in gold or foreign currencies which, for a time, Germany bought with its increasingly worthless currency, until this gambit too was rejected. By 1923, Germany was unable to pay the assessed $33 million dollars in reparations, and thus, pursuant to the Treaty of Versailles, France occupied the Ruhr district to confiscate coal as substitute payment.

The Treaty also limited the German army to no more than 100,000 men and 4,000 officers, dissolved the General Staff, abolished conscription, forbade paramilitary forces, limited weapons development, and outlawed an air force. Nevertheless, Germany began almost immediately to re-arm in secret with tacit approval from the public who felt the Treaty was little more than an attempt to exclude Germany from economic competition with its rivals Britain and France.

Thus, the 200-strong Army General Staff was reconstituted as a civilian organization focusing on history, surveys and maps, transportation, and statistics, which soon grew to over 500 former military officers working in 57 committees that studied the war, rewrote manuals, reviewed tactics, and devised clever Treaty work-arounds. Police forces expanded, acting as de facto military reserves. When Nazi paramilitary groups became prevalent, they were tolerated because the government believed they could be turned to legitimate state purposes. As early as 1925, an Air Transport School was organized, which was actually a military training organization masquerading as a commercial flying school.

After the Nazis obtained a plurality in the 1932 Reichstag elections, Adolph Hitler skillfully orchestrated his back-room appointment as Chancellor. Thereafter, using his bully pulpit, he openly repudiated the Treaty of Versailles, calling it an "embarrassment" and styling his plans for rearmament as a peaceful Blumenkrieg, or "Flower War." In so doing, while the Great Depression wreaked havoc on the former Entente Powers, Germany enjoyed full employment, re-militarized the Rhineland, and tested its new, advanced weaponry in the Spanish Civil War (1936-1939).

The west viewed all of this with apprehension and mixed feelings. A strong Germany was an effective buffer between a free Europe and an expansionist, communist U.S.S.R. But though Germans hated the Russians, as a result of the Versailles Treaty, they had no love for their ostensible allies in the west.

LEFT At the height of Weimar Republic hyperinflation in November 1923, 1 billion marks were worth 1/40th of a penny.

BACKGROUND Nazi troops and officials celebrate the advent of the *Luftwaffe*, the German Air Force.

PRESSURES MOUNT

BY THE DAWN of the 20th century, Japan had been ruled by the same royal family for over 2,500 years. Their island fortress had protected the Japanese from many foreign invasions, including Mongol king Kublai Khan in the 13th century.

In the 16th century, when missionaries accompanying Spanish explorers arrived, the Japanese rejected Christianity and sealed themselves off from the West. As a result, collective thought remained endemic to Japanese culture and notions of individual moral responsibility failed to take hold.

Japanese religion had long been a amalgam of hearth gods, ancestor worship, Buddhism, and divine rulers. Confucianism arrived relatively late and stratified Japanese society into four groups: samurai, farmers, merchants, and artisans.

The samurai *bushido* ("way of the warrior") code includes chivalry, loyalty, self-sacrifice, and honor, but as the samurai grew in power, so did their brutality. By the beginning of the 20th century, the once noble knights had devolved into gangs of hired thugs, engaging in assassinations and all manner of crimes.

In 1902, aware that without modernization it risked being colonized, Japan signed a treaty to protect British interests in the Pacific. In exchange, the U.K. modernized the Japanese fleet, which proved fortuitous, as two years later, the new Japanese Navy routed the Russian fleet at Port Arthur, taking control of Russian interests in Manchuria, northeast of China. Japan now had a foothold on the Asian continent.

Japan entered World War I on the Allied side, ostensibly to escort Australian and New Zealand forces to war zones, but what it really wanted was German colonies if Germany lost the war. In 1915, it overreached when it attempted to make China a "protectorate," a move opposed by the United States, which punished Japan with an immigration ban.

As the war ended and the world remained unsettled, Japan grew anxious. Its population was exploding and its 70 million people were facing starvation. For a nation without natural resources, expansionism was considered not only necessary, but morally defensible. The German possessions it received as mandates would help but they were not enough. Japan needed *more*.

LEFT Samurai *kabuto* iron and leather helmet with *mengu* faceplate and *yodare-kake* throat guard.

10

SHORTLY AFTER THE WAR, Japan's treaty with the U.K. was scrapped under pressure by the United States, which wanted limits on naval power. A weary world agreed that now that the "War To End All Wars" was over, disarmament was in order. Japan thus managed to get the U.S. to agree to build no military bases west of Hawaii or north of Singapore.

By 1927, Japanese civilian government collapsed, leaving the *bushido*-inspired military to rule without restraint. As part of the "mandates" dividing German territory, Japan received the Shantung Peninsula in China as well as a string of Pacific isles, which only served to whet its appetite for conquest.

Since the Russo-Japanese war in 1904, Japan had controlled Manchuria, primarily through local warlords, extracting coal and mineral ore, as well as foodstuffs from rich Manchurian farmland. It also took control of rail lines in the south, stationing guards along the railway to discourage nearby Chinese troops from meddling in Manchurian affairs.

In 1931, without the knowledge of its own government, the Japanese military staged a bombing of the railway near the town of Mukden. The explosion was so ineffective that a train passed over the track minutes later without incident, but the Japanese military immediately accused the Chinese military of the act and engaged in a full-scale invasion of Manchuria. Within five months, Japan had occupied the entire country, establishing a puppet state it called "Manchukuo."

China filed a formal protest with the League of Nations, which resolved that Japan immediately withdraw its troops from Manchuria. Japan claimed its invasion was an act of self-defense and held its breath, waiting for a military response which never came.

For the Japanese, it was a powerful lesson in the limits of western power.

ABOVE Chinese characters indicate a piece of bomb shrapnel at Mukden. Almost no damage was done to the railway tracks.

BACKGROUND Japanese troops triumphantly enter Tsitsihar, China.

SHORT-SELLING THE FUTURE

THE BOOM-BUST business cycle has been historically self-correcting. But with the ascendancy of concentrated government power and an excess of economic theorists in the 1920s, the belief grew that Adam Smith's "invisible hand of the market" could be controlled. The Great Depression should have put the lie to that mistaken belief, which continues today.

It began in the early 1920s as mass production changed the American economy. Autos replaced horses and mules, freeing up farmland previously sowed with forage, resulting in the over-production of foodstuffs. The Smoot-Hawley Tariff sought to protect farmers, but only food exports were in deficit; America had a trade surplus in manufactured goods.

Politicians also sought to keep the world prosperous by deliberate inflation of the money supply. The Federal Reserve Bank secretly enabled easy credit, increasing the money supply by 60%. It manipulated interest levels, keeping them artificially low to stimulate business investment. America shortly become the world's banker, and foreign governments, many of whom owed the U.S. vast amounts of war debt, were enticed to borrow American money, which was tied to proper behavior on their part.

In short, America's rulers rejected the rational *laissez-faire* choice of free trade and hard money and took the soft political option of protective tariffs and inflation.

The 1920s were a boom decade and economists began to believe they could eradicate the bust portion of the cycle by creating credit through price stabilization. Thus, in 1927 the Bank of England and the Federal Reserve conspired to reduce interest rates, which fueled the final wave of speculation that brought on the stock market crash of 1929. But though U.S. productivity went through the roof in the 1920s (largely because of automobile mass production), prices did not go down as they should have, which revealed that inflation was still present as real wages stagnated and goods remained expensive.

Stock market speculation tipped the economy over the cliff. Instead of traditional "buy low, sell high" stock trades, investors began to "short" the market: borrowing stock from lenders, hoping it tanked, purchasing it outright at the new, lower price, and returning the now less-valuable borrowed stock to the lender, thus generating a profit.

In addition, more than half of all stock investors engaged in "margin" trading in which an investor received up to $9 in purchasing credit for every $1 actually deposited. When short selling caused the market to crash, lenders called in these margin loans, which could not be paid back. Banks failed as debtors defaulted, and bank runs occurred as depositors attempted to withdraw their money. But though prices and income fell, debt stayed high.

At this point, the Federal Reserve should have raised interest rates and quit selling cheap credit. Had it done so, the recession caused by the October 1929 market crash would likely have self-adjusted within a year, just as the 1920 recession did, knocking out the speculative element and leaving sound stocks at their real value.

But the government preferred *stability*.

RIGHT The ticker-tape machine received up-to-the-minute stock prices.

THE ERA OF THE ENGINEER

AT THE END of the October 1929 panic, the market index was at 224, down half from 452. But it was 245 just ten months earlier after a year of steep rises. In essence, it had quickly self-adjusted and found its bottom and a recovery was forthcoming.

But WWI introduced the age of social engineering and newly-elected president Herbert Hoover, nicknamed the "Great Engineer," lived up to half of his moniker. Though the myth about Hoover is that he refused to use government money to reflate the economy after the crash, as Secretary of Commerce in the 1920s he proved himself a corporatist, believing that the state, business, and the unions should work together in gentle but persistent manipulation of market forces to make life better.

By the time he was inaugurated in March 1929, the Depression was already on its way and when Treasury Secretary Andrew Mellon advised him to "liquidate labor, liquidate stocks, liquidate farmers, liquidate real estate, and purge the rottenness from the economy," Hoover refused. Had he done so, unsound businesses would have gone bankrupt and wages would have fallen to their natural level. But for Hoover, high wages were essential, both politically and, in the short term, economically.

He was in fact the first president to use government resources to attempt to override the business cycle. He resumed credit inflation, bullied industrial leaders into keeping wages high, and ramped up spending, running large deficits. Huge public works, including the eponymous Hoover Dam, busied his administration. And though he cut taxes at first, the 1932 Revenue Act imposed a balanced budget, and Hoover then oversaw the greatest tax increase in U.S. peacetime history.

Then the tariffs of the 1920s boomeranged, spreading the Depression to Europe. By 1931, a whole slew of European banks had failed, forcing debt-repudiation and pulling the U.K. off the gold standard. American exports to Europe vanished and her policy of foreign loans as a substitute for free trade collapsed. Foreigners lost confidence in the dollar and began pulling out their gold. As a result, there were 5,000 American bank failures in 1932 alone. Landlords could not collect rent and so could not pay their taxes; lack of taxes caused city revenues to collapse, bringing down the relief system and services. Schools closed. Malnutrition plagued the big cities.

In the 1932 election, Franklin Delano Roosevelt carried all but six states. The basically strong American economy was already righting itself and what good financial news there was was immediately dubbed the "Roosevelt Market." And after one month in office, FDR had America drinking legal liquor again, an immense boost to morale.

Having no economic philosophy of his own, FDR largely tinkered with Hoover's ideas. His agriculture policy raised farm incomes but also raised food prices and thus delayed the recovery. And he upped Hoover's ante on public works, spending $13 billion, putting many to work. But public works created no lasting economic engine.

FDR was in tune with the 1930s, which repudiated the virtues of capitalist enterprise and embraced those of collectivism, and he was easily re-elected in 1936. His appeal to the young, to progressives, and to intellectuals survived his abandonment of New Deal innovations in 1938 and his retreat into the hands of metropolitan party machine bosses, who ensured his re-election in 1940 and 1944.

ABOVE Outgoing president Herbert Hoover rides with his successor Franklin Delano Roosevelt in the inauguration day parade.

FIGHTING THE LAST WAR

SHORTLY AFTER THE ARMISTICE, 3 million American servicemen were released from active duty under the premise that future wars with major powers, except possibly Japan, could be avoided by maintaining a minimum defensive military strength, avoiding European entanglements, and using American good offices to promote peace. For the next 20 years, those who watched international events had an uphill battle to keep American armed forces ready for the next, some said inevitable, war.

In 1920, the National Defense Act trimmed the Army to 300,000 men and narrowed its mission: to defend America and her territorial interests only. Within a few years the Army was slashed to just 132,000 troops—smaller than Romania's armed forces.

For the next 15 years, the Army focused on retaining personnel rather than on procuring new equipment. As a result, training was often done on Indian War-era posts with WWI equipment. The Reserves and the National Guard battled forest fires, floods, improved harbors, and delivered air mail. President Roosevelt even ordered Army Chief of Staff General Douglas MacArthur to staff the Civilian Conservation Corps (CCC), a New Deal make-work project, with Army officers to oversee young men left jobless by the Depression, effectively grinding Army officer training to a halt.

In 1922 , the U.S., U.K., and Japan agreed to freeze construction of new capital ships (battleships and carriers) and six years later the U.S. and France signed a treaty renouncing war as an "instrument of national policy," each nation promising to reduce its army to a level sufficient only to oppose direct aggression.

But beginning in the early 1930s, Japan seized Manchuria and renounced its arms treaties, Adolf Hitler came to power in Germany, and Italy invaded Abyssinia (Ethiopia). In response, Congress passed the 1935 Neutrality Act, which embargoed all war parties. In 1936, Spain erupted in civil war and in 1937 Congress renewed the Neutrality Act to include civil wars. Japan then invaded China. The world did nothing.

When Germany annexed Austria in 1938, even the sleepiest politicians woke up. FDR ordered the drafting of war plans and increased the Army to over 500,000 men, including the Reserves and National Guard units.

Against this backdrop, Army modernization had crept slowly forward. The Garand M1 semiautomatic rifle was adopted, replacing the 1903 Springfield. Motorization finally retired horse-drawn artillery. The mobile 105-mm howitzer cannon was developed. Light and medium tanks were designed to support infantry assaults. Lastly, Army divisions were reduced to three infantry regiments instead of the traditional four, decreasing their overall size to little more than half of that of their WWI counterparts, but enhancing their mobility and firepower.

It was, however, too little, too late.

RIGHT The "Brodie" or "Doughboy" helmet used by British and U.S. infantry in WWI. Germans called it the "salad bowl."

KEYSTONE B-3A

Following troubled development in the 1920s, the Army eventually acquired this 75-foot wingspan bomber. Though its performance was only marginally better than its WWI counterparts, it was safer and more reliable. It had a crew of five and a 4,000-pound payload. The last biplane ordered by the Army, it served until 1940.

DOUGLAS Y1B-7

This gull-wing design was the first monoplane given the "B" (bomber) designation. With retractable gear, its semi-monocoque (a combination of stressed skin and internal ribs) construction held a crew of four and 1,200 pounds of bombs. Though it could outrun period fighters, it never went into mass production.

MARTIN B-10

Its revolutionary all-metal airframe, enclosed cockpit, rotating gun turrets, retractable landing gear, internal bomb bay, and full engine cowlings became the standard for bomber designs for decades. Though it was faster than any fighter, it was eclipsed the very next year by

BACKGROUND French cavalrymen gaze up in wonder at a British Airco DH.4 bomber, one of the most successful aircraft of WWI. Almost 7,000 were built.

15

1935
BOEING B-17

B-17G Flying Fortress

Aircraft Type: Long-range heavy bomber.
Powerplant: Four 1,200-hp Wright R-1820-97 Cyclone 9 turbocharged radial piston engines.
Maximum speed: 287 mph at 25,000 feet.
Range: 2,000 mi. with a 5,500 lb. bomb load.
Weight: empty 36,000 lbs; loaded 65,500 lbs.
Armament: 13 .50-caliber machine guns in dorsal, ventral, chin, and tail twin turrets; single dorsal, cheek, and aft beam positions.
Payload: 5,500 lb.
Crew: 10
Dimensions: Span: 103 ft. 9 in.
Length: 74 ft. 4 in.
Height: 19 ft. 1 in.
Wing Area: 1,420 sq. ft.

THE XB-17 ("X" for experimental) eclipsed all predecessors. It was a relatively fast, high-flying, long-range bomber with heavy defensive armament.

Boeing Aircraft, with only 600 employees, spent $400,000 of its own money developing the Model 299 prototype, which rolled out of the factory in 1935. A reporter, counting the plane's thirteen bristling .50-caliber machine guns , whistled low and called the aircraft a "flying fortress." Boeing quickly trademarked the name.

Though the prototype crashed at the air trials in Dayton, Ohio, due to the test pilots' failure to remove the control surfaces gust lock, the Air Corps was so impressed with the design that it ordered 13 aircraft for "service testing." Turbocharger issues delayed the first deliveries until January 1939, but in July 1940 the Army ordered 517 B-17s. Prior to the attack on Pearl Harbor, however, fewer than 200 B-17s were in service.

The B-17 fought in every theater of WWII, but, starting in 1943, won immortality in its epic daylight battles against the Luftwaffe in European skies.

Its sleek good looks, durability, pleasing flight characteristics, and reliable Wright engines gave it the reputation as the best bomber of the war. However, as heavily armed and armored as it was, its speed, range, and payload necessarily suffered.

By mid-1942, Army Air Force Commanding General Henry "Hap" Arnold, noting that high-altitude box formation bombing—a Fortress speciality over Europe—was unnecessary in the vast distances of the Pacific, decided to replace all B-17s in the theater with a faster bomber with almost twice the payload and a longer range, just as soon as it became available.

It would be a year before this newcomer entered the fray and won the Pacific War.

Yes, we can build one...
...one an hour.

I want an aircraft that will
fly the skin off any rivals.

Nothing short of right is right.

I have a sneaking hunch that
the Davis formula is worth a try.

A wing surface is no more
inert than a buzz saw.

THE STARS ALIGN

DRIVEN TO GREAT HEIGHTS

REUBEN HOLLIS FLEET, born 6 March 1887 in Washington state, had adventure in his blood. His forebear Henry Fleet captained the ship that brought John Smith and the first colonists across the Atlantic to Jamestown, the first permanent English settlement in North America. Reuben's father was a civil engineer and founded the city of Aberdeen, WA.

Even as a boy, "R.H." (he hated being called "Rube") had limitless energy. He raised chickens and worked in a shingle mill. As a teenager in military school, he captained the debate team, wrote poetry, played football and, at six-feet tall, was center on the basketball team. He competed in six track events.

After graduation he taught school in his home town of Montesano, "thrashing" misbehaving boys, working as a night janitor, and keeping his father's abstract company's books. Married with two small children, he joined the National Guard, invested in timber tracts, and raised oysters. When the Guard sent him to San Diego on duty, Fleet fell in love with the city, promising himself he'd return one day.

In 1914, friend and former lumberman Bill Boeing arranged for Fleet's first airplane ride. Fleet fell in love with airplanes. That same year war in Europe broke out and Fleet believed America would soon join the fray. But it wasn't until early 1917 that he lobbied for and received a National Guard appointment for flight training in San Diego. Around that same time, President Wilson read a secret telegram in which Germany invited Mexico into the war as its ally, promising to help Mexico recover the territories of Texas, New Mexico, and Arizona from the U.S. Wilson made the cable public and Congress declared war.

Reuben Fleet had taken his first flying lesson the day before. After graduation, he was sent to Washington, D.C. to serve under Col. Henry "Hap" Arnold, setting up primary flight training schools nationwide. Next he oversaw the creation of the Air Mail system and then returned to California to train cadets in Sacramento. They flew **Curtiss JN-4D**s, the famous **"Jenny"** biplane, which was nearing the end of its life as a trainer.

When the war ended, Fleet asked to be put in charge of developing a successor to the Jenny. Instead, he was placed in charge of the Army's aviation contracts and got a close-up look at every new aircraft acquired by the Army from its civilian contractors, most of which he managed to fly himself.

Returning Bill Boeing's favor, he signed the purchasing order hiring Boeing to build a new Army pursuit biplane. Fleet also funded the development of the turbo-supercharger, which used hot engine exhaust gases to drive a compressor which pumped pressurized air into the engine induction system.

He was 34 years old.

LEFT To commemorate the advent of Air Mail, a stamp featuring the Jenny was printed. In 100 stamps the aircraft was printed upside down. In 2007, a single stamp sold for almost $1 million.

LUCK FAVORS THE PREPARED

DAYTON-WRIGHT CHUMMY / TW-3

CONSOLIDATED MODEL 1 CAMEL / PT-1 TRUSTY

CONSOLIDATED MODEL 2 CAMEL / PT-3 HUSKY / NY-2

FOLLOWING THE WAR, the Army's budget was drastically reduced. Like many officers, Fleet was informed that he could stay in the service with a reduction in rank and pay or he could leave. Bypassed for the job of overseeing new trainer aircraft development, Fleet opted for the latter and began entertaining employment offers from Boeing, Curtiss, and Gallaudet, aircraft manufacturers he'd dealt with as Air Service contract supervisor.

Largely forgotten today, during WWI Gallaudet was a prolific builder of airplanes and was interested in developing the trainer Fleet knew the Army would buy. But upon investigation, Fleet discovered that Gallaudet was nearing insolvency. However, their work force and design team were first-rate.

Dayton-Wright Airplanes (which had produced under license the famed de Havilland DH.4 bomber) had been purchased by automotive giant General Motors. They had some aircraft designs Fleet liked, including an all metal side-by-side seat biplane trainer, the "Chummy." But Dayton-Wright was under government investigation for contract shenanigans and GM was ready to dissolve the company.

Reuben Fleet was never one to miss an opportunity, so, in 1923, exactly 20 years after the Wright brothers' first heavier-than-air flight, he made an immense gamble: he would purchase aircraft designs from Dayton-Wright and lease the Gallaudet factory and employ its workers under the auspices of a new, aptly-named company, Consolidated Aircraft Corporation, which would be capitalized with just $60,000, a quarter of which Fleet himself would contribute. That same year, Fleet's gamble was rewarded when the Air Service signed a $200,000 contract with Consolidated for 20 model **TW-3** trainers, an updated military version of the Chummy.

Though the seating arrangement of the TW-3 with the instructor sitting next to the student was superior for training purposes, the lack of visibility out of the cockpit made the arrangement inconvenient and dangerous. A tandem version was built, called the **"Camel"** because of a hump between the two cockpits. Fleet himself redesigned the radiator and removed the engine cowling to improve performance and visibility.

The Camel had enviable flight characteristics. It was able to pull itself out of a spin in just 1.5 turns. No one else in the industry knew how Fleet did it and he told no one his secret, which was that the upper wing (which contained the fuel tanks) was situated forward of the lower wing leading edge. The centrifugal force of the fuel in a spin lowered the nose, allowing the aircraft to exit the spin by itself.

In 1924, as he had long planned, Fleet entered the Air Service's competition to replace the Jenny, and won an order for 50 Camels. The plane was given the military designation **PT-1 "Trusty."** Though considered rather ugly, Fleet called it the "best, strongest, flying-est trainer on the world."

In 1928, Consolidated delivered 300 radial engine versions of the Trusty called the **PT-3 "Husky,"** half of which went to the Army and half to the Navy. Famed test pilot Jimmy Doolittle made the world's first fully instrumented blind flight in the Navy NY-2 version later that same year.

In just six years Consolidated Aircraft Corporation had become the largest volume manufacturer of airplanes in the U.S.

FLEET BEATS DEFEAT

WHILE THE ARMY tightened its belt after WWI, the Navy saw its budget grow. Believing that Japan was the only threat on the horizon, the Navy got carriers, destroyers, and cruisers. It also wanted flying boats.

At Consolidated, Chief Engineer Isaac "Mac" Laddon had already designed the Boeing PB-1 biplane flying boat and knew the ropes. On 28 February 1928, Consolidated won the Navy contract, designating its entry the **XPY-1*** and nicknaming it the "**Admiral**."

The pilots sat in an open cockpit, and the navigator-bombardier in another open cockpit further forward, with a radio operator and mechanic-gunner astern. With a 100-foot wingspan and 62-foot length, it had nearly the same dimensions as the later Model 32, which would become the famed B-24 Liberator.

The Admiral was first demonstrated to the Navy on 22 January 1929 to great acclaim. But Fleet was stunned when the Navy put his design up for competitive bids and Martin Aircraft won the right to build the Admiral. "Of course they won," complained Fleet bitterly. "They had no development costs to factor into their bid."

Never one to accept defeat, Fleet tweaked the Admiral design for civilian use, calling it the "**Commodore**." It carried 32 passengers and a crew of three. Prohibited from competing with airlines in the continental U.S., Fleet obtained air mail and passenger route contracts between the U.S. and South America,, creating the New York, Rio & Buenos Aires Line, which instantly became the world's longest commercial airline.

Pan American Airlines competed with Consolidated in the overseas passenger and air mail markets, but the Post Office wanted just one U.S. company carrying the air mail. It chose Pan Am. NYRBA turned over its contracts and merged with Pan Am.

It wasn't all bad news for Reuben Fleet, however. Pan Am wound up purchasing 14 Commodores, allowing Consolidated to recover its Admiral development costs and more: in 1930, Consolidated sold 309 airplanes, more than any other American aircraft manufacturer.

CONSOLIDATED MODEL 16
PY COMMODORE

* Note on naming: "X" stood for experimental, "P" for patrol, "Y" for Consolidated ("C" had already been taken by Curtiss Aircraft), and "1" because it was Consolidated's first model in this type.

CONSOLIDATED MODEL 28
PBY CATALINA

TESTING SEAPLANES on the ice-covered Niagara River in wintertime was challenging and Reuben Fleet pondered relocating Consolidated from Buffalo, NY, to warmer climes. Ever since his National Guard duty in 1911, Fleet had dreamed of living in temperate San Diego. On 29 May 1933, the Consolidated board voted to move to California and two years later shipped its entire factory in 157 railroad cars, moving into new buildings constructed on Lindbergh Field, adjacent to the harbor.

The next generation seaplane, the Model 28 **XP3Y-1 "Catalina,"** was the most successful flying boat ever designed and the culmination of everything Fleet and Chief Engineer Isaac Laddon had learned over the years. It was a streamlined, all-metal monoplane powered by two 825-hp Pratt & Whitney "Twin Wasp" engines built into the leading edge of the wing, which was supported by a pedestal that also served as the flight engineer station. Laddon cleverly designed the floats to fold up after take-off and transition into outboard wing tips. He also developed a gas-tight wing fuel cell, which saved a half-pound of fuel per gallon.

So impressive were the Catalina trials that the Navy redesignated the aircraft from P (patrol) to PB (patrol bomber) and paid $6 million for 60 copies, the largest contract awarded by the U.S. government since WWI. The Catalina was now known as the PBY-1.

Just a year later, the Navy ordered another 50 PBYs and awarded Consolidated the contract to build an even bigger seaplane with four engines and a payload of up to 12,000 pounds. The resulting **XPB2Y-1 "Coronado"** made its maiden flight on 17 December 1937, the same day the 100th PBY Catalina was delivered to the Navy.

Unfortunately, the Coronado suffered from design issues, a range under half that of the Catalina, and a tripling of cost per unit. Used primarily at low altitudes as transports and hospital ships, Coronados saw only limited combat in the Pacific during WWII.

CONSOLIDATED MODEL 29
PB2Y CORONADO

Consolidated's lean years were ending. Despite the fact that the country was in the depths of the Great Depression, Consolidated now had over 3,700 employees, four times the number it employed just two years ago. Under orders from the government, it even licensed Russia to build 150 Catalinas.

KITCHEN TABLE REVOLUTION

DAVID R. DAVIS was heir to a paper company fortune and thus he had the freedom of tracing Lewis & Clark's journey, navigating a motor boat down the eastern seaboard, and visiting the Panama Canal... all when he was still a teenager. So when he found his passion—aeronautic design—he was used to acting on his own and taking risks.

At 23, he bought his first airplane, a Jenny. When his mother died and the family fortune became his, he partnered with Donald W. Douglas to form the Davis-Douglas Aircraft Corp., producing the "Cloudster," a thick-winged airplane that was the first design to carry its own weight in payload. But it didn't sell.

He worked for Bendix developing the first non-mechanical variable pitch prop, but when the stock market crashed, he left to pursue his longtime dream of the "perfect" wing. The performance of a wing is determined not only by its *plan* form—the silhouette you see when looking up at a plane's wing in the sky—but also by its *airfoil*, the shape of the cross-section showing the curvature of the wing's surface.

Historically, wings had been designed by the cut-and-paste method, then tested in wind tunnels and re-shaped by hand according to performance. Davis wanted a mathematical formula that expressed air-flow dynamics. Unfortunately, without an engineering degree, he lacked the math skills (particularly calculus) to accomplish this formidable task. Besides, aerodynamicists had already established that 90% efficiency of an airfoil was the practical limit. Reduction of that last 10% of drag was impossible due to irreducible resistance and skin friction. Or so they said.

But from his time at Bendix, Davis knew that a propeller was nothing more than a spinning airfoil. If not for the aircraft controls preventing it, a wing would spin in the air like a rolling pin, creating a slipstream behind it as it moved forward, the rounded leading edge tapering to the trailing edge, a length called the "chord." Thus, the shape of the wing actually begins with a perfect circle, like a drop of water that elongates into its characteristic tear-drop shape as it falls through the air. Only in this case, the teardrop is falling horizontally. And the more smoothly the teardrop moves through the air, the less drag is generated. It occurred to the young inventor that maybe that last 10% was reducible after all.

"A wing surface is no more inert than a buzz-saw," posited Davis. "It whips the tar out of the airstream, smashing its resistance and converting it into work for the plane. That, stripped of elegant technical terms, is *lift*."

By 1931, Davis had perfected his formula and applied for a patent. Owing to the formula's purely mathematical basis, it took the U.S. Patent Office three years to issue the patent for his "Fluid Airfoil."

Patent in hand, Davis was now ready to test his theory. Unconventional as ever, he built a three-foot wooden airfoil segment and mounted it on the roof of a friend's car, racing along southern California highways in the still air of dawn at speeds of up to 90 m.p.h., calibrating the results with home-made instruments. When he was satisfied that his theories were correct, he asked his friend Walter Brookins (the Wright brothers' first civilian student pilot) to contact someone for him.

"Who would you like to see?" asked Brookins.

"There's only one man who will understand what I'm trying to do," said Davis. "He's a hard-headed maverick who knows airplanes. Reuben Fleet."

CONSOLIDATED MODEL 31
P4Y CORREGIDOR

REUBEN FLEET PUT down the formula-filled page and studied his slight, bespectacled visitor. "I'm a practical engineer, Mr. Davis," he said, "not an aerodynamicist. I can't make heads or tails of this." He looked at Chief Engineer Isaac Machlin Laddon, who had picked up the page and was concentrating on it. "What do you think, Mac?"

Laddon furrowed his brow. "There's outside chance he's on to something here."

Davis beamed, shook hands with his hosts, and left. Fleet turned to Laddon. "If this thing pans out, can we use it on the Model 31?"

"We've already designed a wing for that bird," said Laddon. "Changing it now, based only on an amateur's theory, is a big risk. We'll have to build a wing section and test it."

Fleet shrugged. "We're financing this new ship ourselves. What's another $40,000?"

In his L.A. apartment, Davis began work on an eight-foot wing section of laminated mahogany according to the plan form requirements for the Model 31, a new flying boat designated the **XP4Y "Corregidor."** It would have a deep hull, cantilever wings, "wet wing" fuel tanks, and be powered by two 2,000-hp Wright R-3350-8 Cyclone 18 engines. It would be very heavy and would need all the lift it could get.

At CalTech in Pasadena, the wing section was placed in the wind tunnel. Tests usually took a day and results were usually available in a week. Two weeks went by and still no report. Davis thought they were getting the run-around, but in actuality the airfoil efficiency was clocked at 102%, exceeding the theoretical maximum, so the engineers took their wind tunnel apart, recalibrated their instruments, rebuilt the tunnel, and ran the test again. Same result. A third time, too.

After three long, agonizing weeks, the report finally arrived:

> The most startling of the Davis wing results is the air-foil efficiency factor showing that the slope of the lift curve is very nearly the value of 2 Pi, which is predicted by perfect fluid, thin airfoil theory. Practically all of the wings [we've] tested had values between 0.87 and 0.92. The remarkably high value for the Davis wing (0.983) is probably a variation of boundary layer with angle of attack, but no real explanation for it has yet appeared.

Laddon whistled through his teeth. "An almost perfect laminar flow. Unbelievable."

"Glad he's already under contract," said Fleet. "Let's put his wing on the Model 31."

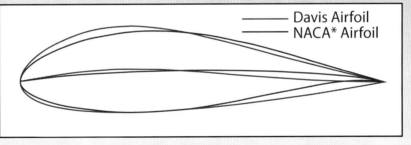

— Davis Airfoil
— NACA* Airfoil

Construction on the new plane, informally dubbed the "Pregnant Guppy," began in July 1938. A commercial version with a crew of five would carry 52 passengers in a double-decked interior, have fully-retractable beaching gear, and a singular high-aspect-ratio wing (a wing whose span is long compared to its chord, or width). But the Davis wing looked too insubstantial to carry such a bloated fuselage and many engineers working on the aircraft had serious doubts.

But on 4 May 1939, test pilot Bill Wheatley lifted the Guppy off the water in San Diego bay in a take-off run as short as if he'd been on dry land. It had an incredible rate of climb and handled so well he actually dove on the factory and powered away in a steep climbing turn. "It's a pursuit plane!" he exulted.

As David Davis's formula had predicted, the Fluid Airfoil bettered all existing wings by 20%. The Model 31 reached an easy top speed of 275 mph as compared with the Catalina's 175 mph. It had a cruising range of 3,500 miles and a ceiling of over 21,000 feet. The only thing it didn't have was a bomb bay.

Reuben Fleet and Isaac Laddon would see to that.

* The National Advisory Council for Aeronautics (NACA) was the forerunner of NASA.

AIRCRAFT AMALGAM

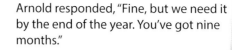

IN A FIERY 1935 SPEECH, Adolf Hitler boldly declared that his Luftwaffe was as powerful as the Royal Air Force. The U.K. and France paid little heed. After all, Britain had the world's largest navy and France the biggest army. Unfortunately, the coming war would be won in the air.

In March 1938, on the pretext of guaranteeing a unification referendum, Germany annexed Austria. In September, British Prime Minister Neville Chamberlain returned from Munich with Hitler's solemn promise that Germany had no further European territorial claims, calling it "peace in our time." There is still debate about whether Chamberlain was a credulous fool or was wisely trying to buy time for Britain to prepare for inevitable war.

President Roosevelt heard Hitler's speech and asked Maj. Gen. Henry "Hap" Arnold, Chief of Army Air Forces, to report on America's readiness. Arnold discovered that only thirteen copies of the Boeing B-17 bomber had been delivered and none had high-altitude capability.

So in early 1939, Arnold called up his old friend and asked Reuben Fleet if he could build B-17s. Fleet did some research and called Arnold back. "I won't build the B-17," he said flatly. "There isn't enough work at Boeing to divide between us and besides, the Fortress is an old design. I can build a better bomber."

Arnold responded, "Fine, but we need it by the end of the year. You've got nine months."

The Army then issued Type Specification C-212 for a bomber with a 3,000 mile range, 35,000 foot ceiling, 300 mph maximum speed, and an 8,000 pound payload. Only Consolidated's Model 31 Corregidor flying boat even came close to the requirements; no one else had anything on the drawing board.

Fleet called project manager Frank Fink into his office and told him he needed a mock-up that answered the Army specs within two weeks. Fink blanched. "Don't worry," said Fleet. "We'll use the Davis wing and the twin tail from the Model 31, the engine nacelles from the PBY Catalina, and design a fuselage with two bomb bays, each the size of the B-17's bomb bay."

Fink still had the wood mock-ups for the Catalina and the Corregidor. Working day and night, he and his crew delivered the new Model 32 mock-up on time.

Model 32 was designated the XB-24 and was loaded with innovations: flexible internal wing fuel bladders of Dupont Duprene (neoprene), corrugated roll-up bomb bay doors, Fowler flaps, an 8,000 lb. payload, tricycle gear, and, like the Catalina, powered by the reliable Twin Wasp engine—four of them.

When Reuben Fleet looked over the finished XB-24 prototype, he stopped abruptly near the plane's nose. "Doesn't look right. Too stubby! Add three feet forward of the windshield. You'll have a better looking plane."

By February wind tunnel tests were complete and in late March, Consolidated signed a $2.9 million Army contract for 7 YB-24s. Though the San Diego factory was already working overtime churning out the popular PBY Catalina, the bomber prototype was prioritized. In August, the Army ordered an additional 38 bombers to be designated B-24As.

On 1 September 1939, Luftwaffe Stuka dive bombers attacked the Polish Air Force, destroying most of it on the ground, a prelude for Wehrmacht's devastating *blitzkrieg*, or lightning war. Two days later, the United Kingdom and France declared war on Germany.

World War II had begun.

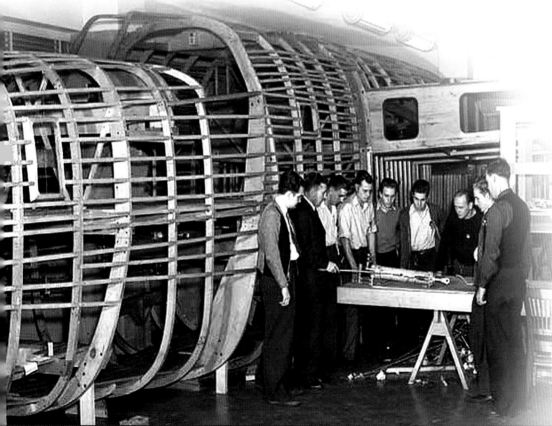

ABOVE Reuben Fleet first met H.H. Arnold in 1917 when Fleet was in pilot training on North Island in San Diego Bay. Capt. Arnold was the supply clerk.

HAPPY NEW YEAR

CONSOLIDATED MODEL 32
XB-24

IT WAS A TYPICAL winter's day in San Diego on 29 December 1939 when the **XB-24** was rolled out of the hangar and onto the tarmac at Lindbergh Field: sunny and cool—perfect flying weather.

Test pilot Bill Wheatley settled into his seat. As always, Isaac Laddon was with him. Reuben Fleet watched as the big bird rolled down the runway, his $1 million gamble riding on David Davis's "paper" wing.

Emotions were riding high. Both Jimmy Doolittle and Charles Lindbergh had recently returned from Germany and reported grimly that Hitler was planning for war. France and the U.K. were eager to order hundreds of this new bomber. *If* it flew.

Wheatley advanced the throttles and the XB-24 lifted smoothly off the runway and into the sky. The heavy plane was incredibly responsive and soon he was pushing the aircraft to its limits, swooping, diving, stalling—there was apparently nothing it could not do.

Reuben Fleet heaved a sigh of relief and Frank Fink grinned. Employees cheered as news photographers clicked away.

It would be portentous new year.

RIGHT Consolidated test pilot William "Bill" Wheatley in the cockpit, sporting his trademark engineer's cap.

A GOOD START

OF COURSE IT WASN'T PERFECT. No aircraft is, especially on its maiden flight. In testing, the Model 32 had a number of issues that needed to be resolved:

- Pitot tubes (which measure air pressure and generate air speed readings) were relocated from the outboard wings to either side of the fuselage nose for greater accuracy.
- Landing gear were redesigned to retract fully into the wing, thus reducing drag.
- Fleet was right: the nose *was* too stubby. Three feet were added to move the center of gravity forward as required by the tricycle gear.

- Engine nacelles were redesigned to include air inlets to increase engine cooling.
- The R-1830-33 engines lacked turbochargers, necessary for high-altitude bombing runs.
- There was no armor plating to protect the crew.
- Cruising speed was 27 mph less than the Army's 300 mph requirements.
- Wing slots, which promote low-speed handling, were unnecessary and drag-inducing.
- The tail span was increased two feet for better rudder authority.

ABOVE When testing was complete, the XB-24 was outfitted as a corporate transport and given a new designation (XB-24B) and a new serial number (39-680).

THE PRODUCTION POOL

FOUR MONTHS AFTER the XB-24 test flight, Norway, Holland, Luxembourg, and Belgium all toppled like dominoes to the German juggernaut. Winston Churchill replaced the hapless Neville Chamberlain as British Prime Minister. In America, President Roosevelt appealed to Congress for 50,000 military aircraft a year.

In San Diego, Reuben Fleet authorized a $3 million plant expansion, bringing Consolidated's factory to 1.5 million square feet. It wasn't enough as PBY Catalina orders continued streaming in and the first B-24 orders were received.

In December 1940, aircraft and automobile manufacturers met in Washington, D.C., where George Mead of Roosevelt's National Defense Council laid down the law: the automobile industry would start producing aircraft Ford would be teamed with Consolidated on the B-24 heavy bomber; GM with North American on the B-25 medium bomber; and Chrysler with Martin on the B-26 medium bomber. Factories would be built in the safety of the country's interior, supervised by the aircraft manufacturers but owned by the government.

Fleet cautioned against this creeping nationalization of the aircraft industry, saying he didn't have the personnel to run these new plants but if expansion was necessary, he could train men in San Diego who could work in the new plants. As an incentive, the Army financed a 1.6 million square foot expansion to Consolidated's San Diego plant.

The aircraft builders soon discovered that the President had already promised aircraft plants to Tulsa, OK, and Fort Worth, TX. North American Aircraft, in Dallas, TX, would also build B-24s.

Fleet designed the Ford plant at Willow Run, near Ypsilanti, MI. As it neared completion, he visited and rode down the assembly line in an electric cart with Ford's production manager, Charlie Sorensen. As they neared the far wall, the building took a 90 degree right turn and continued another 600 feet. "This wasn't in my layout," said Fleet.

"This facility is in Washtenaw County," said Sorensen. "If we continue straight, we'll enter Wayne County, which has property taxes five times those of Washtenaw."

"But the plant is owned by the government and it pays no taxes," said Fleet.

"But after the war is over, Ford hopes to own it and operate it as an airplane plant."

Fleet thought, *Ford's been out of the airplane business for 13 years, since the days of the Trimotor. Here you are holding his hand and teaching hundreds of his people the modern aircraft manufacturing business and he's already telling you he is going to buck you when the war is over.*

Ford went on to produce over 8,000 B-24s at Willow Run, completing one every 59 minutes.

But it produced no more aircraft after the war.

ABOVE In one of the most famous factory photos of WWII, scores of B-24Ds move down the mile-long assembly line at the $45 million, air-conditioned Ft. Worth, TX plant.

REFINING THE PROTOTYPE

YB-24 / LB-30A

AFTER THE XB-24's maiden flight, Laddon got to work correcting its weaknesses, but the war in Europe was raging and both France and Britain had ordered hundreds of the new bomber. The USAAC itself ordered seven copies, to be designated the "**YB-24**" ("Y" is Consolidated's assigned letter in U.S. military aviation nomenclature).

But France fell in June 1940 and the Royal Air Force (RAF) inherited the order, asking that the USAAC's seven aircraft be diverted to England as soon as possible. Agreeable, the Army Air Corps retained one YB-24 for testing and delivered the other six, designating them **LB-30As***. The USAAC wasn't disappointed; it would rather wait for the next batch of improved B-24s. (Remember, America was not yet in the war.)

When the six LB-30As arrived in November 1940, the British were thrilled but the aircraft had one major flaw: the wing fuel tanks were not self-sealing, a must for combat over the Continent. The RAF thus outfitted them to ferry air crews between Scotland and Canada to pick up combat aircraft. Beginning in May 1941, the LB-30As (now with British serial numbers AM258-AM263) transported hundreds of aircraft from the Americas into the maelstrom of the European war.

When the LB-30As arrived, the British asked Fleet if the bomber had a nickname. "**Liberator**," he said proudly. "Because this airplane can carry destruction to the heart of the Hun, and help liberate those nations under Hitler's yoke." (The name had been coined by his children's governess, Edith Brocklebank, who was British.)

WITHIN SIX MONTHS, the British took delivery of another 20 aircraft, called the **B-24A "Conversion"** by Consolidated but dubbed the **LB-30B** by the USAAC. The British called it the "**Liberator Mark I**" and gave serial numbers AM910-AM929 to the batch. The only surviving copy today is the Commemorative Air Force's *Diamond Lil,* which suffered gear damage during its flight to the east coast in the spring of 1941. After repairs, it returned to San Diego where it was borrowed for use by Consolidated as a wartime transport.

Like its predecessor, the Mark I did not have self-sealing fuel tanks. It was outfitted with .30-caliber machine guns in the States but the British added a 20-mm Hispano cannon under the nose, air-to-surface radar (note the dorsal antenna array in the photo at right), and stocked the bomb bay with depth charges.

By summer 1941, Mark Is went to work with the No. 120 Squadron of the RAF Coastal Command as sub-chasers, their 2,400 mile range locating German U-boat packs hiding in the North Atlantic just beyond PBY Catalina range, and thus freely wreaking havoc on Allied shipping. During their tenure, Mark Is were credited with sinking 8 submarines.

One of the B-24A Conversions was among the first U.S. aircraft to see combat during the war. While being equipped for high-altitude photo reconnaissance of Japanese bases in the central Pacific, it was parked at Hickam Air Field on O'ahu, Hawaii. On 7 December 1941, it was destroyed in the surprise attack that finally brought America into the war.

B-24A / LB-30B / LIBERATOR MARK I

* "LB" stands for Land Bomber. "30" represents Consolidated's 30th design proposal (as opposed to model number—such as the Model 32—which progresses to a physical prototype).

THE LIBERATOR GOES TO WAR

ON THE HEELS of the 6 and 20 aircraft already ordered, in early 1941 Britain ordered another 140 Liberators. The country had weathered the Battle of Britain and it was by air power alone that it had been saved from conquest by the German Luftwaffe. No one need remind them they were susceptible to attack from the skies.

But in December 1941, America was attacked at Pearl Harbor and the Army requisitioned half of the British order for itself, designating 70 planes as **LB-30s**. A Martin top machine gun turret was in place as well as a hand-held tail gun. The first American-flown Liberator saw battle in January 1942, hitting an airfield in Java.

The "**Liberator Mark II**"s arriving in England in August 1941 were the Mark I design, upgraded with the three-foot nose extension that Fleet had recommended and, finally, self-sealing fuel tanks. The Brits installed power turrets in the tail and dorsally on the fuselage aft of the wing. Each turret held four .303-caliber Browning machine guns. Four more were mounted in the nose, belly, and at the two waist windows. Curtiss Electric propellers spun on the latest P&W R-1830-61 Twin Wasp engines.

Winston Churchill's private transport, *Commando*, was a Mark II.

Marring the roll-out was the Mark II's first test flight, in which a loose bolt left over from the manufacturing process somehow jammed the elevator control in the up position, causing the aircraft to stall and crash into San Diego Bay, killing pilot Bill Wheatley and all others aboard.

LB-30 / LIBERATOR MARK II

WITH THE WORLD at war and hundreds of orders, both foreign and domestic, rolling in, it was time to finalize the assembly line. Thus, the **B-24C** was a "breakdown" aircraft whose purpose was to iron out manufacturing bumps for the next variant of Consolidated's heavy bomber, the B-24D, which would be produced in the thousands.

Just nine B-24Cs were delivered to the Army Air Corps in early 1942; none saw combat. They had the now mandatory self-sealing fuel tanks and supply lines, as well as turbo supercharged Pratt & Whitney R-1830-41 engines, which required that the round cowl be reshaped as an oval with "cheek" scoops on either side for directing cooling air to the turbo supercharger and intercooler.

In addition, it was the first USAAC Liberator to boast a top turret, which had two .50-caliber machine guns and was located in the flight deck. It also received the three foot nose extension Fleet had recommended when he first saw the XB-24 prototype.

Consolidated designed and built its own turret, the A-6, and installed it in the tail position. Two machine guns were mounted in both the waist and nose. A floor-mounted "tunnel" gun protected against enemy fighters aiming at the aircraft's underbelly. Though the tunnel gun was notoriously inaccurate, it provided a measure of comfort to the aircrews and a moment's hesitation to attackers.

B-24C

B-24D / LIBERATOR MARK III

THE BEST OFFENSE...

THE DESIGN AND TESTING phases were over. Five factories of the Liberator Production Pool were gearing up. It was time to mass-produce the B-24 on a war-footing schedule.

The RAF's early experience with the Liberator revealed weaknesses in range and armament. For the **B-24D**, six more fuel cells were added to the outer wing sections, increasing capacity by 450 gallons and adding 200 miles to the range. The latest Twin Wasp engines (R-1830-43) were incorporated.

The Liberator's 8,000 lb. bomb bay was unequaled by any other aircraft, but its defensive armament was woefully inadequate. The Martin A-3 top turret, first appearing in the "C" model, was a great boost, as was the Consolidated A-6 tail turret, but the ship's belly and the nose were nearly defenseless.

So the first "D"s featured a single machine gun mounted in a socket in the greenhouse nose. Soon, two more guns were placed to each side in the "cheeks," but their limited field of fire and the cramped conditions in the nose with a bombardier, navigator, and gunner begged for a better solution. The nose gun was therefore lowered and fired by the bombardier from a prone position. In later versions, it was fixed and rigged to be fired by the pilots. All stop-gap solutions.

But as is the case in most new technologies, the users themselves discovered the solution: ground crews of the 5th Army Air Force in Australia grafted a Consolidated A-6 tail turret from a wrecked bomber onto the nose of a new B-24D, and it proved a brilliant success. Soon Consolidated engineers were doing the same.

The belly tunnel gun of the B-24A was resurrected, then replaced with a periscope-mounted twin-gun remote Bendix turret, which, in addition to being inaccurate, gave the gunners motion sickness. The tunnel gun was tried again but was finally scrapped altogether in favor of the Sperry A-13 ball turret that had proved so indispensable to the B-17. It was imported to the Liberator with one major improvement: instead of a fixed mount (exposing the gunner to all manner of gruesome outcomes should turret damage prevent his exit during flight), it was mounted on an armature that retracted hydraulically into the aircraft.

Finally, for the first time, .50-caliber Browning AN/M-2 air-cooled machine guns were mounted in the waist windows, directly opposite each other at first and then staggered because the gunners grew tired of colliding with each other during battle.

The RAF went further: Rockets were mounted on some of their "**Liberator Mark III**"s and "Leigh Light" carbon arc spotlights, capable of illuminating a surface vessel with 90 million candles, hung from wings.

These improvements turned the Liberator from a high-flying, long-range, heavy payload-delivery aircraft into an unequaled and fearsome weapon of war capable of delivering its message anywhere in the world. Over 2,700 were built in San Diego, Fort Worth, and Tulsa.

It was the first Liberator variant to be flown into combat by U.S. Army crews.

ABOVE An early B-24D—one of thousands of this variant to come—makes its first flight over San Diego Bay, the white scallop-roofed Consolidated factory in the background.

HITS AND MISSES

THE NEXT THREE iterations of the Liberator were B-24Ds with minor changes. The **B-24E/"Liberator Mark IV"** was the first to be built in its entirety at Willow Run after a troubled process in which Ford had trouble adapting from steel automotive to aluminum aircraft materials and training its underskilled workers to build to the exact specifications of the aircraft industry. By the time the assigned lot of 800 aircraft were complete, they were obsolete and relegated to stateside service only.

A B-24D was converted into a **B-24F** and used to test thermal de-icers on wing leading edges instead of the standard inflatable rubber "boots."

The **B-24G/"Liberator Mark V"** was built by North American Aviation in Dallas, TX, from "knock-down kits" (subassemblies) provided by Ford. The 26th copy marked a nose redesign for the Liberator family. The old "greenhouse" nose was replaced by a nose featuring an Emerson power turret with two .50-caliber Browning M-2 machine guns. The Liberator *finally* had the forward defensive armament it needed.

B-24E / LIBERATOR MARK IV

B-24H / LIBERATOR MARK VI

FORD FINALLY GOT it right and produced the **B-24H/"Liberator Mark VI,"** which was a hit with crews. It was the first model to feature a factory-fitted nose turret, the electronically-powered Emerson A-15. The North American nose design was improved, giving the bombardier a three-panel window for sighting bomb runs. A new, taller "high hat" top turret, the Martin A-3D, gave the gunner better visibility. And the waist windows now enclosed with Plexiglas, the guns projecting through them, was warmly received at 25,000 feet.

But pilots were torn. They liked the new left aileron tab which made the aircraft easier to fly. They also appreciated that the reduction in aircraft weight yielded another 1,000 feet of altitude. But they didn't like Ford's "coffin seat," an armored shroud around their seats that prevented the wearing of a parachute and hindered emergency exit. In Europe, where most Hs flew, the 8th Air Force replaced the coffin seat with a "flak curtain" across the rear of the flight deck.

FROM THE START, the Navy had been flying **PB4Y-1**s (B-24Ds in Navy livery) in anti-submarine patrols in both the Atlantic and the Pacific, but the aircraft flew poorly at low altitude and speed. A new version, the **PB4Y-2 "Privateer,"** with a single vertical tail, had been wind-tunnel tested and found to better satisfy the Navy's needs.

Other changes included a seven foot fuselage extension between the cockpit and the wing to accommodate a flight engineer's station and the use of non-turbocharged P&W R-1830-94 engines. A second top turret was added aft of the wing and waist guns were placed in oval-shaped blisters, and the ball turret was eliminated, a savings of 1,500 lbs.

By the end of the war, Consolidated had delivered over 700 PB4Y-2s to the Navy, which used them into the 1960s. Some flew as fire fighting bombers for years after that.

PB4Y-2 PRIVATEER

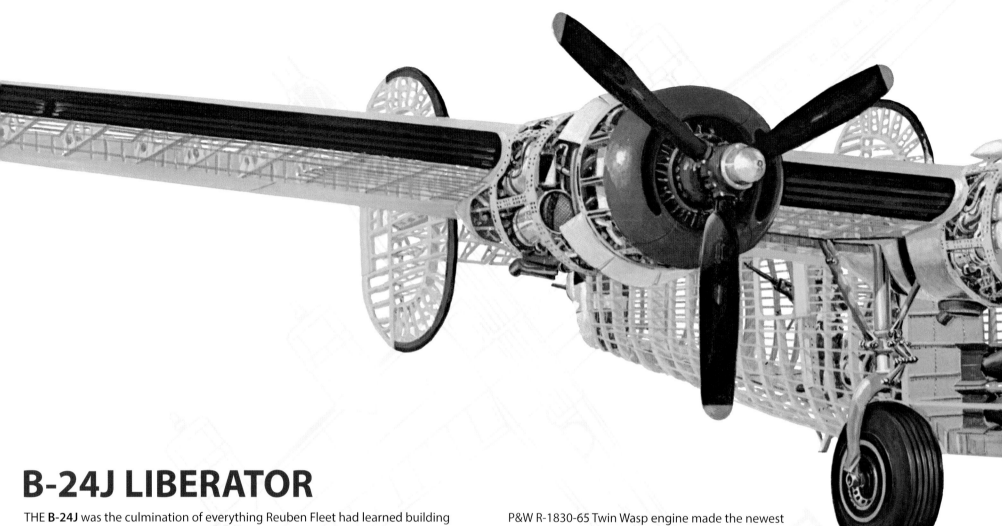

B-24J LIBERATOR

THE **B-24J** was the culmination of everything Reuben Fleet had learned building aircraft over the last twenty years. The J was the first Liberator built concurrently in all five factories (San Diego, Tulsa, Ft. Worth, Dallas, and Willow Run) and in greater numbers than any other B-24 model—6,676 copies.

Incorporating most B-24D elements, the biggest change was the nose turret, first tested in Ft. Worth and then improved at Willow Run. But the preferred Emerson A-15 turret was slow off the assembly line, so most Js received a modified version of Consolidated's own A-6 tail turret for use in the nose until Emerson caught up on their backlog.

The Martin A-3D "high-hat" top turret and staggered and enclosed waist gun positions of Ford's popular H model were not incorporated into the San Diego J model, but an improved C-1 autopilot and the M-9 Norden bombsight, along with ducted hot-air de-icing (as opposed wing leading edge rubber "boots"), and the turbo-supercharged

P&W R-1830-65 Twin Wasp engine made the newest Liberator the standard by which all other models, before and after, would be judged.

The hurried nine-month concept-to-prototype rush had cost the kind of design niceties so evident in the sleek Boeing B-17, which had years of languid development. And the outbreak of the war just weeks before the XB-24's first flight meant even more pressure for engineers, fabricators, factory workers, war planners, and air crews alike.

Nevertheless, the Liberator reigned as war's most indispensable aircraft. It was produced in greater numbers than any other American military aircraft—*up to and including today*—18,482, half again as many as B-17s built, proof of the Army Air Force's confidence in the ungainly, slab-sided, flying boat with the skinny wing.

B-24J Liberator

Aircraft Type: Long-range heavy bomber.

Powerplant: Four 1,200-hp Pratt & Whitney R-1830-65 turbo-supercharged radial piston engines.

Maximum speed: 290 mph at 28,000 feet.

Range: 3,300 mi. with no load; 2,100 mi. with load.

Weight: empty: 36,500 lbs; loaded: 65,000 lbs.

Armament: 10 .50-caliber machine guns in dorsal, ventral, nose, and tail twin turrets; single aft beam positions.

Payload: 8,800 lb. maximum.

Crew: 10

Dimensions: Span: 110 ft.
Length: 67 ft. 8 in.
Height: 18 ft.
Wing Area: 1048 sq. ft.

The Liberator flew in every war theater: pummeling Rommel in North Africa; engaging in devastating daytime high-altitude strategic bombing raids over northern Europe; braving costly low-level attacks over Romanian oil refineries; crossing the vast distances of the Pacific to pound the Japanese homeland; seeking and destroying evasive U-boats in the frigid North Atlantic; patrolling the Americas from Argentina to Alaska; and carrying precious fuel and supplies across the Himalayas to supply our Chinese allies.

By any standard, the Liberator truly was *the* aircraft workhorse of World War II.

THE NEXT GENERATION

MODEL 33 XB-32

B-32 DOMINATOR

B-36 PEACEMAKER

FIVE YEARS AFTER the 1935 rollout of his B-17 heavy bomber, Bill Boeing signed a contract with the Army Air Corps for the B-29, a super-heavy bomber predictably called the "Superfortress," which, after costly delays (its development costs exceeded those of the Manhattan Project), finally saw combat over Thailand in June 1944. That same day in 1940, though he was just beginning Liberator fabrication, Reuben Fleet also signed a contract for an **XB-32 "Dominator"** prototype, a design similar to the B-29 should it fail to deliver.

The B-32 was based on the B-24, with a twin tail, the Davis wing, but with a longer, rounder fuselage. It would use the same Wright 3350 Cyclone radial engines as the B-29 and would also be pressurized and feature remote-controlled machine gun turrets, though the novel idea of placing backward-firing machine guns and a 20-mm cannon in the outboard engine nacelles was Fleet's alone, as were using reversible-pitch propellers on the inboard engines.

But Fleet, like Boeing, ran into problems. Like the B-29, the B-32 engines were prone to catching fire due to poorly-designed cowls. But unlike the Superfortress, the Dominator's twin tails were insufficiently stable for the 100,000 lb. aircraft and had to be replaced with 20' vertical fins. But when the bugs were worked out in 1944, the USAAF ordered 1,500 B-32s.

Beginning in June 1944, B-29s started hitting Japan. Their raids were so successful that when the first Dominators were delivered in September, they were relegated mostly to photo reconnaissance missions of previously-hit targets. Sadly, the last American airman to die in WWII, photographer's assistant Sergeant Anthony Marchione, was killed when Japanese fighters attacked his B-32 *Hobo Queen II* on such a photo run.

On 8 September 1945, after building just 118 copies, Consolidated's contract for the B-32 Dominator was cancelled. No exemplars exist today.

IN 1940, THE U.K. almost lost the Battle of Britain and U.S. war planners began to ponder how America could fight Nazi Germany with no European allies. The Army needed a truly intercontinental bomber with a 5,700 mile flight radius, a 275 mph cruising speed, a 450 mph top speed, and a 45,000 foot service ceiling. Both Boeing and Consolidated submitted proposals, but Consolidated's **B-36 "Peacemaker"** was chosen by the Army Air Force in 1941.

It was a revolutionary design: powered by 6 giant 28 cylinder Wasp Major radial engines mounted in a pusher configuration (later supplemented by four turbojets that sparked the slogan "six turnin' and four burnin'"), 19 foot propellers, a wingspan of 230 feet (twice that of the Liberator), and a payload heavier than an entire B-17 Flying Fortress: 86,000 lbs.

Though production delays led to the Navy calling it a "billion-dollar blunder" (mostly because it took money away from Navy projects, including its wish-list of "super carriers"), the Army Air Force stuck to its guns. The Peacemaker first flew in 1946 and until it was replaced by the Boeing B-52 Stratofortress in 1955, served as America's foremost nuclear deterrent due to its ability to carry the first-generation atomic device, the huge Mark 16 hydrogen bomb.

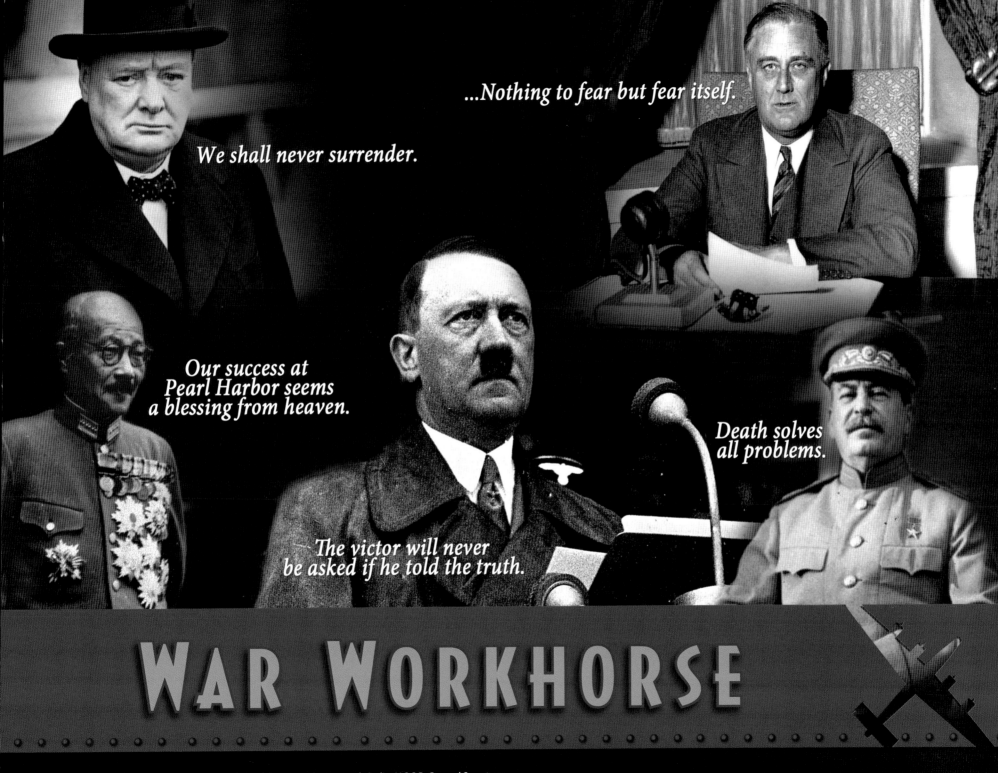

...Nothing to fear but fear itself.

We shall never surrender.

Our success at
Pearl Harbor seems
a blessing from heaven.

Death solves
all problems.

The victor will never
be asked if he told the truth.

WAR WORKHORSE

THE FLOWER WAR

SINCE THE END WWI, the Allies had occupied the Rhineland, Germany's industrial center bordering France, Luxembourg, and Belgium, in order to ensure the payment of reparations and to prevent German rearmament. France even took in-kind payment of coal from the Saar, located in central Rhineland. Angry German workers staged strikes and work slow-downs in opposition.

In 1929, due to the Weimar Republic's hyper-inflationary money policy, Germany threatened to default on all reparation payments unless the Allies left the Rhineland immediately. Accepting what they saw as inevitable, both Britain and France left in 1930, five years early. In March 1935, German troops marched into the Rhineland, greeted enthusiastically by the mostly German population.

Hitler expected opposition to his militarization of the Rhineland, but when none came, he began his next conquest. The Austrian parliament had a small but virulent Nazi contingent. In early March 1938, on Hitler's orders, Austrian Nazis staged riots in an attempt to seize power from the fascist-Catholic government, whose Chancellor, Kurt von Schuschnigg, showed surprising backbone when he agreed to immediately submit the question to the population in a plebiscite.

Hitler was outraged and threatened invasion, ostensibly to ensure that the referendum was orderly and democratic but in reality he knew the Treaty of Versailles prohibited Austro-German unification and that the Austrian public would likely defeat the proposition.

Then Schuschnigg shocked Hitler again by cancelling the plebiscite and resigning,

and Austrian President Wilhelm Miklas refused to appoint Hitler's candidate for Chancellor, Nazi Arthur Seyss-Inquart.

On the evening of 11 March 1938, Hitler ordered the invasion to commence at dawn. At 10:00 pm a forged telegram sent in Seyss-Inquart's name asked for German intervention and after midnight, President Miklas resigned himself to the inevitable and installed Seyss-Inquart as Chancellor, who immediately transferred all power to Germany.

The next day Wehrmacht troops entered Austria to enforce the *Anschluss* ("joining") and the plebiscite was held under their watchful eye, the only issue put to Austrians being a ratification of what had already occurred: the commandeering of Austria by Nazi Germany.

Generally, German troops were received as liberators and showered with Nazi salutes and cheers. The *Blumenkrieg*, or "flower war" Hitler had so skillfully engineered had conquered a country without firing a shot. England and France made noises but did nothing.

BACKGROUND German troops triumphantly cross a bridge over the Rhine River, gateway to Germany's traditional industrial heartland, which has been occupied by the Allies since WWI.

APPEASEMENT FOR OUR TIME

IT WORKED IN AUSTRIA, so Hitler used the same strategy in Czechoslovakia, a nation formed from the ashes of the Austro-Hungarian Empire that had, living in an area called the Sudetenland just inside its border, millions of Germans—25% of the population—who also wanted unification with Germany, which was clearly becoming, under Hitler's management, an economic and military powerhouse. But Czechoslovakia was a democracy, and this complicated Hitler's plan.

So in June 1938, he began by pressing for autonomy for German Czech citizens and then quickly upscaled his demands for transfer of the Sudetenland to Germany. At Munich in September, British Prime Minister Neville Chamberlain and French PM Edouard Daladier acquiesced to Hitler's demands after extracting his promise that Germany had no further territorial aspirations in Europe. Chamberlain returned to England, calling the Munich Agreement "peace for our time," but because no Czech official was present during the negotiations, the Czechs themselves bitterly derided it as "About us, without us!"

Like clockwork, in March 1939, Germany invaded Czechoslovakia. When the British government did nothing, Winston Churchill noted angrily that with the annexation of Czechoslovakia—which had one of the biggest and most advanced militaries in Europe—Hitler had gained another twelve Army divisions, again without firing a shot.

Predictably, within two weeks of marching into Czechoslovakia, Hitler denounced his 1934 nonaggression pact with Poland, which also had a large German population. Britain responded by giving Poland a weak guarantee of support.

In August 1939, Joachim von Ribbentrop of Germany and Vyacheslav Molotov, foreign ministers of Germany and the Soviet Union respectively, met in Moscow to sign a mutual non-aggression pact. Historian Paul Johnson put it this way: "As the tipsy killers lurched about the room, fumblingly hugging each other, they resembled nothing so much as a congregation of rival gangsters who had fought each other before, and might do so again, but were essentially in the same racket," toasting an agreement which included a secret protocol for dividing up Poland, Finland, Romania, Lithuania, Latvia, and Estonia into "spheres of influence."

His eastern flank now secure, one week later, on 1 September 1939, Adolf Hitler invaded Poland.

Two days later, the U.K. and France, finally startled fully awake, declared war on Germany. World War II had begun.

ABOVE   British Prime Minister Neville Chamberlain triumphantly returns from Munich.
BELOW   Foreign Minister Joachim von Ribbentrop (L) celebrates the pact with Josef Stalin (R).

THE CALM BEFORE THE *STURM*

AS RECENTLY AS MAY 1939, France made a solemn promise to the Poles that if Poland were invaded, France would come to their rescue, but when Germany invaded Poland on 1 September, France merely reinforced its Maginot Line defenses bordering Germany. What followed for the next nine months has been dubbed the "Phony War," in which, for the most part, only minor skirmishes between the major powers occurred.

Following their new German ally, on 17 September, the Soviets invaded Poland from the east, speeding its collapse. That same day, *Unterseeboot* (U-boat) U-29 sunk the British aircraft carrier HMS *Courageous,* which was on patrol off the Irish coast, killing over 500 crewmen. A month later, German *Luftwaffe* fast bombers Junkers Ju-88s attacked British warships in a Scottish fjord, but were driven off by British Supermarine Spitfires.

At the outset of the war, Sweden, Norway, and Denmark declared themselves neutral and Sweden continued selling ore to Germany which was loaded onto German ships in Norwegian ports. In October, War Cabinet member Winston Churchill proposed mining Norwegian waters to force the ore shipments to detour through the North Sea, where they could be intercepted by the Royal Navy. His plan was rejected.

On 30 November, the Soviets demanded that for Leningrad's "security," Finland must cede border territory. Finland refused and the USSR invaded. Though the Soviets outnumbered the Finns 3 to 1, for several weeks the Finns repelled them in what became known as the "Winter War."

Plans by France and Britain to come to Finland's aid were scuttled when Sweden, Norway, and Denmark refused passage of Allied troops through their countries.

Finally, in March 1940, the Finns were forced to sue for peace, turning over 11% of their territory and 13% of their economy to the Soviet Union.

Shortly thereafter, proof that no appeasement goes unpunished, Hitler ordered the invasion of Norway and Denmark, claiming that Germany was actually "protecting their neutrality against Franco-British aggression."

On 7 May, after a heated debate in the House of Commons, Prime Minister Neville Chamberlain narrowly survived a no-confidence vote. Three days later, Germany invaded France, Belgium, and the Netherlands. Chamberlain immediately resigned and King George VI appointed prescient firebrand Winston Churchill Prime Minister.

The Allies finally had a leader to match the intelligence and cunning of their enemy.

ABOVE Finnish soldiers show their determination fighting for their homeland.

"OUR FINEST HOUR"

ON 14 JUNE 1940, German troops entered Paris unopposed and a week later the French signed an armistice that was tantamount to surrender. The country was split into a northern occupied zone and a southern unoccupied rump under the Vichy Regime, which, though officially neutral, was actually a puppet state.

The same week, Winston Churchill gave his "Finest Hour" speech, saying, "The Battle of France is over. The Battle of Britain is about to begin. Hitler knows he will have to break us in this island or lose the war."

Hitler had already tasked *Reichsmarshall* Herman Göring with breaking British will, beginning with the Royal Air Force (RAF), before the implementation of "Operation Sea Lion," his invasion plan for the British Isles, scheduled for 15 August. Therefore, one week after Churchill's remarks, the Luftwaffe began small-scale probing attacks, armed reconnaissance flights, and mine-laying sorties over England.

On 4 July, the air war began in earnest as both sides attacked military targets on either side of the English Channel. The battle soon escalated to an all-out air war pitting Germany's 750 Me-109 and Me-110 fighters escorting 1,300 He-11 and Do-17 bombers, along with 300 Ju-87 dive bombers against only 700 Spitfire and Hurricane fighters. Dogfights raged throughout July. British early warning radar helped the RAF better their adversaries in most engagements. By early August, Germany had lost 300 planes, the British half that many.

On 13 August, Göring upped the ante with *Aldertag* ("Eagle Day") as the Luftwaffe staged massive attacks on RAF airfields. For the next week, almost continuous aerial combat followed; the sky literally rained spent .303-caliber cartridges. Young British pilots were thrown into combat with just a few hours flying time. A week later, an emotional Churchill addressed the House of Commons, praising the courage of the RAF: "Never in the field of human conflict," he declared, "has so much been owed by so many to so few."

A few days later, Luftwaffe bombers strayed off course and dropped their ordnance on London. The next day, in retaliation, British aircraft bombed Berlin. An outraged Hitler vowed to lay waste to British cities and authorized the *Blitz*, the all out destruction of civilian population centers in England. More than 2,000 Londoners were killed or wounded on the first night, 7 September. On 14 November, more than 400 German bombers attacked Coventry, killing 568 civilians and injuring 1,400 others, but the steely and stoic determination of the British population inspired the RAF to fight even harder.

The Blitz continued for another six months but Britain did not fall.

ABOVE The Supermarine Spitfire Mk. 1 fighter, powered by the Rolls-Royce Merlin engine, was a worthy adversary to the German Messerschmitt Bf-109.

THE TONNAGE WAR

THE LONGEST CONTINUOUS military campaign of the war pitted German U-boat submarines against Allied merchant and military convoys. German Vice Admiral Karl Dönitz had devised a "wolf pack" tactic in which several U-boats would spread out in a line across an enemy's projected course. When a target was sighted, they would attack *en masse*, usually at night.

Within hours of the declaration of war, *Unterseeboot* U-30 sank the British ocean liner SS *Athenia*, killing 128 passengers and crew. Britain summarily blockaded German ports; Germany did likewise, but though Germany was largely self-sufficient, the British Isles imported a million tons of material per week. A blockade meant starvation and the end of the Allied cause.

Between September 1939 and February 1943, U-boats ruled the North Atlantic. In particular they called June 1940 the "Happy Time" in which they sunk 270 Allied ships.

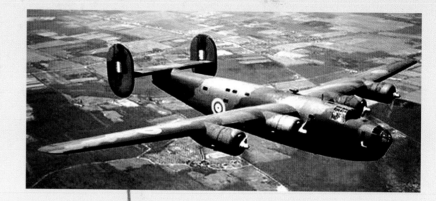

When the U.S. entered the war, escort groups got bigger and could spare sub-chasers and still protect the convoy. Improvements in radar, depth charges, and code-breaking eventually neutralized the U-boat threat, but before naval escorts were widely available, air protection was limited to shore-based aircraft, leaving a large "air gap" between Greenland and Iceland where the subs lay in wait for the convoys.

Which is why Lord of the Admiralty Winston Churchill fast-tracked the transfer of the French B-24 bomber order to the RAF. When the first 20 Liberator Mk. 1s arrived in June 1941, their range and payload made them a natural choice for Coastal Command's U-boat patrols. Twelve of the aircraft were designated **Liberator GR Mk. I** ("General Reconnaissance") and were outfitted with radar, 20-mm cannons, and high-intensity Leigh Lights. Assigned to No. 120 Squadron based in Iceland, the VLRs (Very Long Range), as they were simply called, began closing the air gap. Their effectiveness was inarguable: after they began patrolling off Canada in 1942, only one convoy ship was lost.

Prior to the Liberator Mk. IIs arriving in England, there were only 18 Liberator Mk. Is patrolling the Atlantic sea lanes. Nevertheless, they alone were responsible for sinking 5 U-boats.

By the time Dönitz called off the U-boat attacks in May 1943, 3,500 merchant ships and 175 warships had been sunk by wolf packs in 100 convoy battles and almost 1,000 single-ship encounters.

After the war, Churchill wrote, "The Battle of the Atlantic was the dominating factor all through the war. Never for one moment could we forget that everything happening elsewhere, on land, at sea or in the air depended ultimately on its outcome."

ABOVE The *Kriegsmarine* (German Navy) U-boat war badge honored gallantry in action.

BARBARIC BARBAROSSA

OPERATION BARBAROSSA ("Red Beard") was named after the 12th century German king who became Emperor of the Holy Roman Empire, whom legend claimed would return to restore Germany's greatness.

He would need more tanks.

By 1940, Stalin was the only world leader who still believed Hitler's promises, and he clung to the 1939 Nazi-Soviet Pact for days after the Wehrmacht invaded the U.S.S.R. in the biggest military offensive in history, and also the greatest betrayal. Hitler had never intended to keep his word; his race-destiny views were intractable. His war on the West was one of conquest, but his war on the East was total war to exterminate communism and expand German territory. And he had to rid himself of Stalin before America got into the war.

So, on 22 June 1940, three German army groups invaded the Soviet Union with clear objectives: The North Group, under Wilhelm von Leeb, would take Leningrad, the U.S.S.R.'s primary naval base. The Center Group, under Fedor von Bock, would capture Moscow, the heart of the Soviet Union. The South Group, under Gerd von Rundstedt, would obtain Kiev, Ukraine's grain fields, and the industrial Donbass region.

Most German gains were made in the first two weeks. Within a week the Baltic States and Belarus had fallen and by 1 September, the Germans were shelling Leningrad. By 14 July, Moscow was within grasp, but Hitler redirected von Bock's panzer (armored) divisions to Kiev, where three Soviet armies were trapped.

But an early winter and long, largely horse-drawn supply lines soon bogged down the offensive. Soviet General Georgy Zhukov turned Leningrad into a fortress of pillboxes and trenches and when Hitler pulled von Leeb's panzers, he could only lay siege. Near Moscow, eight Red Armies were destroyed and 673,000 prisoners were taken, but when the temperature dropped to -60° F, the offensive stalled.

A spring 1942 Red Army offensive pushed Axis troops back from Moscow. Now that America was in the war, supplies reinforced the Soviets and they regained ground in Ukraine.

The war ground on in 1943. The Soviets finally got a rail line into Leningrad and broke the siege. Moscow remained inviolate. And in Ukraine, though German troops reached Stalingrad on the Volga River, the offensive was exhausted. Russia was simply too big to conquer.

Barbarossa should have succeeded. A crusade against Russian Bolshevist communism would have been supported by the West, the countries Hitler had already subjugated, and many Russians who had suffered for a generation under Stalin's brutality. But Hitler was not a liberator. Like Stalin, he was an enslaver. The accident of race made them opponents and pitted their regimes against each other.

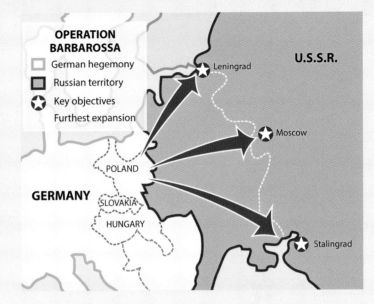

OPERATION BARBAROSSA
- ☐ German hegemony
- ◼ Russian territory
- ★ Key objectives
- ⸱⸱⸱ Furthest expansion

U.S.S.R.

Leningrad

Moscow

POLAND

GERMANY

SLOVAKIA

HUNGARY

Stalingrad

In the end, 3 million Germans faced 4 million Red Army soldiers along a 2,900 mile front that stretched along the Volga River from Archangel in the Arctic to Astrakhan on the Caspian Sea. There was untold death and devastation. Germany lost 1 million soldiers; the Soviets 26 million soldiers and civilians. 70,000 towns and villages were razed to the ground. And, notwithstanding the U.S.S.R.'s losses, because it kept Germany occupied in the East, allowing the Allies to win in the West, when the war was over, it was permitted to subjugate the whole of eastern Europe under the crushing yoke of communism.

BACKGROUND German 28th SS Volunteer Grenadier Division troops examine destroyed Soviet tanks near Riga, Latvia.

DAY OF INFAMY

FDR AND CHURCHILL saw it coming, but they were mistaken as to *where*. They thought Japan's first strike outside of China on behalf of its "Greater East Asia Co-Prosperity Sphere" would be southward, in Malaysia, Hong Kong, or the Philippines. They never imagined the Japanese would have the temerity to attack America in its own backyard.

Besides, the radar on Opana hill on northeast O'ahu was working well. Early on 7 December 1941 it spotted a cluster of aircraft, but everyone thought these were a flight of B-17s on their way to the Philippines. Besides, America had broken the Japanese code—we would have heard if something was up. Problem was, we heard nothing at all, and this made CIC Pacific Fleet Admiral Husband Kimmel anxious. A quarter of his fleet had been transferred to the Atlantic for convoy escort duties, and the PBY Catalinas tasked with patrolling Hawaii's perimeter had been on the ground for three days for routine maintenance.

Admiral Isoroku Yamamoto, architect of the attack, was Harvard-educated, spoke perfect English, and had traveled extensively in America. He knew Japan could never match the military might of the United States, but he also believed in Japan's destiny and when the Emperor green-lit his attack plan, he obediently put it into action.

Thus, before dawn, 183 aircraft took off from Yamamoto's task force and headed southwest, tuning their radios to KGMB in Honolulu, using the station playing Hawaiian music as a homing beacon, where they heard the weather report: visibility good, wind out of the north at ten knots.

At 7:48 am, Zero fighters cleared the Koolau Ridge. All was quiet below; Honolulu was literally asleep this Sunday morning. Though the military had been on alert for a week, the alert ended Saturday, and soldiers and sailors alike were on liberty. In the harbor, air-tight ship doors stood ajar to air out musty compartments before the day's inspection. At Wheeler Field, P-40 fighters sat defenseless, their gas tanks empty and their ammo secured in the armory.

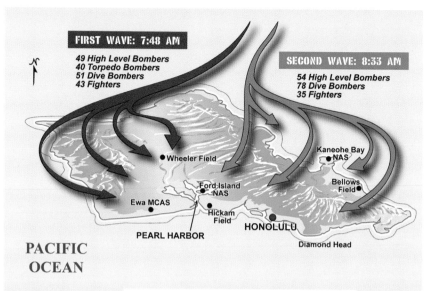

FIRST WAVE: 7:48 AM
49 High Level Bombers
40 Torpedo Bombers
51 Dive Bombers
43 Fighters

SECOND WAVE: 8:33 AM
54 High Level Bombers
78 Dive Bombers
35 Fighters

Wheeler Field

Kaneohe Bay NAS

Ford Island NAS

Bellows Field

Ewa MCAS

Hickam Field

PEARL HARBOR

HONOLULU

Diamond Head

PACIFIC OCEAN

O'AHU ATTACK WAVES

Squadron commander Mitsuo Fuchida was the first to see Pearl Harbor. No alarm had been sounded; not an answering plane was in the air. Keying his radio mike, he confirmed to his fellow pilots that their attack was a complete surprise, shouting, "Tora, Tora, Tora!"* and banking sharply toward Battleship Row as he thumbed the bomb release catch aside.

For America, World War II had finally come home.

* "Tora" means "tiger," the code word that initiated the bombing and strafing runs on Pearl Harbor.

BACKGROUND Sailors aboard a motorboat attempt to rescue a survivor from the USS *West Virginia*, crippled by Japanese torpedoes.

RUNNING WILD

The Japanese heavy cruiser *Mikuma*, struck by SBD Dauntlesses, lists to port

DESPITE THE SINKING of the USS *Lexington* and the crippling of the *Yorktown* carriers in the Coral Sea in May 1942, Admiral Isoroku Yamamoto needed a knockout blow to finally eject the U.S. Navy from the Pacific. And he knew the exact place: Midway. He would draw America's carriers to the tiny atoll and eliminate them once and for all. He did not know, however, that American cryptographers had broken the Japanese naval code and knew his plans down to the date and time. Admiral Chester Nimitz, CIC of the Pacific Fleet, planned an ambush of his own, ordering the carriers *Enterprise* and *Hornet* to join the repaired *Yorktown* northeast of Midway to lay in wait for the Japanese.

Yamamoto scheduled his Midway operation to coincide with the Army's Aleutian Island invasion, which would draw U.S. ships in the area. The battleship *Yamato* would then land 500 troops at Midway, supported by the carriers *Akagi, Kaga, Soryu,* and *Hiryu.* But it was the Japanese who were surprised as, before dawn on 3 June, a PBY Catalina spotted the task force 500 miles southwest of Midway. Nine B-17s attacked from Midway but did little damage.

Early the next morning, fleet commander Vice-Admiral Chuichi Nagumo launched his initial attack, sending 72 dive bombers and torpedo bombers, escorted by 36 Zeroes, to Midway. At this point, bad weather northeast of the atoll hid the American fleet, and PBYs were again searching for the Japanese, whom they found just before dawn. Again, Midway-based bombers headed for the task force. F4F Wildcats remained behind to protect the islands, intercepting the incoming strike and getting a shellacking, though they were able to shoot down 7 enemy aircraft.

The Midway runways survived the attack. TBF Avengers detached from the *Hornet* then attacked the Japanese fleet, but were repelled. When an American B-26 nearly crashed into Nagumo's bridge, he ordered all dive bombers to be equipped with bombs to destroy the Midway runways once and for all. The armaments crews were loading bombs when a scout plane reported a large American force to the northeast. Nagumo reversed his order and torpedoes were mounted on the aircraft for an immediate strike against the American ships. But Nagumo's Midway strike force was returning low on fuel and needed to land. Launching the torpedo-laden aircraft would have to wait.

In an air war, thirty minutes is an eternity. During that time, another strike from Midway arrived but did little damage. It was now 0800. Unknown to Nagumo, at 0700 Admiral Jack Fletcher had launched 150 aircraft at the Japanese fleet, which was at the limit of their range. Thus, with no time to form up, they headed piecemeal toward the enemy. TBD Devastators sighted the enemy carriers at 0920, but most were shot down by surface fire or Zeroes; those that weren't launched Mark 13 torpedoes that failed to explode. Despite their failure, their constant attacks prevented the launching of Japanese fighters during the battle.

Just then, three squadrons of SBD Dauntless dive bombers arrived. Japanese aircraft filled hangar decks, fuel hoses snaked across flight decks, and bombs and torpedoes were everywhere. It was tinder waiting for a spark, and beginning at 1022, the SBDs scored direct hits and within eight minutes, the *Soryu, Kaga,* and *Akagi* were all on fire.

Only the *Hiryu* was not hit and it was able to launch its dive bombers, which chased the retreating Americans back to the *Yorktown* and dropped three bombs on her, sealing her fate.

Later that day, the Enterprise launched a final SBD strike at the lone surviving carrier *Hiryu*. Despite being defended by a dozen Zeroes, five bombs hit and left her ablaze. She sank the next day.

Admiral Fletcher knew the U.S. had won a great victory and withdrew. The tables had turned—this was the last time the Japanese would mount an offensive naval battle in World War II.

The hero of Midway, the rugged and maneuverable Douglas SBD Dauntless dive bomber.

BACKGROUND Midway, a 2.5 square mile atoll in the Northern Pacific, has two islands, Sand Island (top) and Eastern Island (bottom).

TEAM OF RIVALS

AMERICA WAS FIGHTING in two hemispheres, and it had already been decided that the European conflict would take priority. Nevertheless, President Roosevelt had two able commanders on the other side of the world: Supreme Allied Commander General Douglas MacArthur presided over the Southwest Pacific from his headquarters in Australia and Admiral Chester Nimitz was tasked with subduing the central Pacific.

Each had a plan to win the war involving "leapfrogging," bypassing heavily fortified areas and concentrating their limited resources on strategically important islands on the road to Japan. But each had a different road map. MacArthur wanted to consolidate the Solomon Islands (safeguarding the U.S.-Australia trade corridor), then isolate the Japanese at Rabaul, New Britain, then move west through New Guinea and retake the Philippines and Okinawa, from which he could attack Japan itself.

Nimitz proposed moving through the Pacific, destroying Japanese outposts when necessary, isolating them when possible, freeing Formosa, then taking airfields in China from which an invasion of Japan could be effected.

FDR wisely approved both plans, primarily because he knew neither strong-willed commander would willingly work under to the other. But though they started out independently, the Army and Navy needed each other. MacArthur could not make his amphibious assaults without prior naval bombardment and Nimitz could not eradicate opposition without boots on the ground, as proven by the bloody Tarawa battle, which required the killing of almost every Japanese defender on the tiny atoll.

And they both needed the Air Force, in particular the B-24 Liberator, the only bomber capable of spanning the vast distances of the Pacific. Thus, General Henry "Hap" Arnold "loaned" out the 5th, 13th, and the 7th Air Forces to both MacArthur and Nimitz for the pre-invasion pummeling of Japanese outposts all across the Pacific, from the Gilberts to China and from Guadalcanal to the Ryukyus.

Progress was slow, but by mid-1944, the President had to choose one or the other's plan: would the invasion of

Japan be staged from Okinawa or China?

Given their political differences, FDR knew he must assuage MacArthur's conservative supporters back home; it was an election year, after all, and the President was running for his fourth term. So MacArthur it was. Nimitz, always a team player, regretfully acquiesced and both men united forces and pressed toward Okinawa, which would be the platform for the invasion of Japan.

It would be the war's deadliest battle.

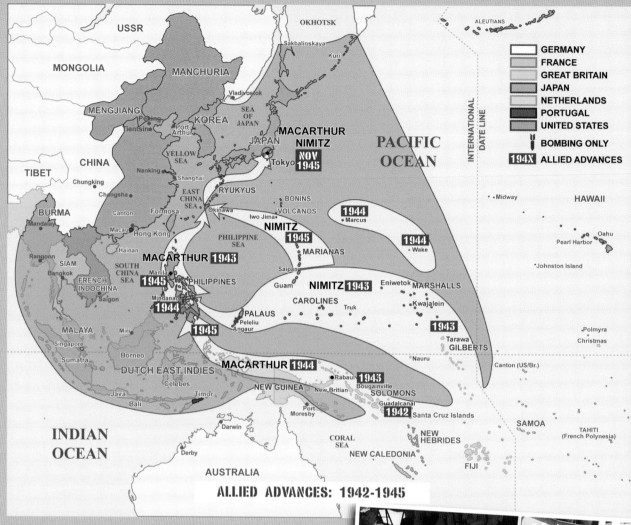

ALLIED ADVANCES: 1942-1945

	GERMANY
	FRANCE
	GREAT BRITAIN
	JAPAN
	NETHERLANDS
	PORTUGAL
	UNITED STATES
	BOMBING ONLY
194X	ALLIED ADVANCES

RIGHT General Douglas MacArthur, President Franklin Roosevelt, and Admiral Chester Nimitz relax in the deck of the USS *Baltimore* at the Pearl Harbor Conference, July 1944.

INTO AFRICA

IT WASN'T LONG before the Liberator got into the war. Following Pearl Harbor, LB-30s were sent to Alaska, Hawaii, and Panama to defend against potential Japanese attacks.

On 10 June 1940, Italy declared war on France and the U.K. Within a week, the British had crossed the Egypt-Libya border and captured Fort Capuzzo, the first of many humiliating defeats for the Italians. Finally, in early 1941, Hitler sent General Erwin Rommel to North Africa to prevent a complete Axis rout. Rommel had early success and advanced into Egypt and the battle seesawed across the desert sands.

In January 1942, three LB-30s joined in the first bombing mission by American-manned Liberators, striking a Japanese aerodrome in the Celebes.

In June 1942, Lt. General Lewis Brereton, commander of the U.S. Army Middle East Forces, formed a B-24 bomb group in Fayid, Egypt, near the Suez Canal. In July, they moved to Lydda, near Tel Aviv, Palestine, where they were joined by the 98th Bomb Group ("Pyramiders").

As Rommel drove the British 8th Army to El Alamein, Egypt, Pyramider B-24s attacked a sea convoy, sinking one of the five tankers supplying the bulk of Rommel's fuel and oil. Over the next few months, they crushed Rommel's chances of capturing Egypt by severing his supply lifeline.

In late October, the 376th Bomb Group ("Liberandos") arrived in Lydda and supported the Allies in the decisive Second Battle of El Alamein, where the Germans, entrenched among 450,000 land mines, were out-fought and flanked by Commonwealth troops, who broke the line and took 30,000 German troops prisoner.

The next week, the Operation Torch landings took place in French North Africa. After a short battle, the Vichy French quit and joined the Allies. During the operation, the Pyramiders and the Liberandos interdicted convoys and disrupted communications.

On 22 November 1942, from an airbase in Gambut, Libya, B-24 Liberators bombed Tripoli, the first Americans to wage war against that city since the U.S. Marines landed there in 1804 to defeat the Barbary Pirates.

UNLUCKY *LADY*

THINGS STARTED OUT BAD then got worse for the crew of *Lady Be Good*, a Liberando B-24D based in Benghazi, Libya. The last to take off in a sandstorm on 4 April 1943, Captain William Hatton soon lost visual contact with the other twelve bombers over the Mediterranean. Nine planes turned back; only four made the seven hour trip to bomb Naples harbor, which was obscured by clouds when they arrived. They aborted.

Hatton then turned south and salvoed his payload. At midnight, he radioed Benghazi, saying his Radio Direction Finder (RDF) wasn't working and asking for a heading, which was given as 330 degrees. Believing he was still north of Benghazi, he naturally used the heading's reciprocal and steered 150 degrees. Unfortunately, he had already passed the coast and was over the vast Calanshio Sand Sea, which at night was as featureless as the ocean. Two hours later, their fuel nearly gone, nine crewmen bailed from the aircraft, which entered a slow, shallow descent, skidding in for a landing sixteen miles further south.

Eight crew members located each other with flare guns and revolvers. The bombardier was not found; his parachute failed to open and he plunged to his death.

The next day, with one canteen of water between them, the survivors began walking north, believing they were near the coast. They were actually 440 miles inland. Marking their path with detritus, they covered seventy miles in three days. On 9 April, three men left the others, who were too weak to continue, promising they would return with help. After another fifty miles, they too succumbed to the heat, cold, and lack of water.

In 1958, a British oil exploration team spotted the wreckage from the air. When a ground crew arrived, they discovered that though the aircraft was broken in two, it was immaculately preserved, with functioning machine guns, a working radio, and food and water. A thermos contained drinkable tea and one of the tires still held air.

Further search revealed the bodies of the three men who went for help. A diary's last entry said simply, *Monday, April 11, 1943. No help yet, very cold nite.*

The bombardier's body was never found.

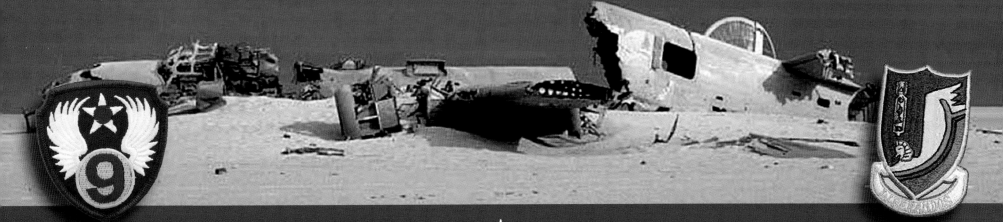

LIBERATOR
OF CONQUERED NATIONS

AVIATION
The Oldest American Aeronautical Magazine

NOVEMBER 1943

Blitz for Blitz

HOW DO YOU LIKE 'EM, MR. HITLER?

The men and women of ALCOA ALUMINUM

before it's **TOO LATE!**

BUY WAR BONDS and STAMPS

"Twelve Zeros jumped the B-24 over Wewak, attacking from all sides. The Jap pilots took advantage of cloud cover... closed in...suddenly attacked through open spots, but could not escape the waist gunners. The Liberator destroyed six of the enemy, returning safely with one engine out and 64 bullet holes."

Army Air Forces report

Give us MORE B-24's

U. S. ARMY OFFICIAL POSTER

THE B-24 LIBERATOR was widely celebrated during the war, as seen in these propaganda posters, magazine covers, and ads. At the same time there was rationing of gas, rubber, and sugar. As a way of financing the war, the government encouraged citizens to buy War Bonds for 75% of their stated value, redeemable in full in ten years.

"It's fortunate for the United Nations the **LIBERATOR** is on our side!"
—ARMY AIR FORCES

ABOVE While the boys were away at war, the girls stayed busy, building the ships they flew in. These remarkable Kodachrome images remind us that their world was as colorful as ours.

BEHIND THE EIGHT BALL

THOUGH FLYING FORTRESSES flew the first American-crewed bomb runs over northern Europe, seven weeks later, on 9 October 1942, Liberators of the 44th Bomb Group joined the fray, hitting Lille on the French-Belgium border.

Decked out with their "Circle-A" tail markings, the 44th "Flying Eight Balls" typified the B-24 Liberator bombing experience over Europe. Before arriving in England, the 44th trained three other groups and sunk U-boats in the Caribbean in its spare time. Its first mission on 7 November 1942 was uneventful, the last mission to be so.

In January 1943, the Group hit U-boat sub pens at Saint-Nazaire on the French coast. In February, on a mission to Dunkirk to sink a German raider, 67th Squadron commander Major Donald MacDonald's B-24D was hit by flak. Stunned, pilot Arthur Cullen looked around. One inboard engine was in flames, the other was simply gone. They were in steep dive. The cabin roof had been torn off. There was no yoke control. MacDonald, bleeding from his stomach, motioned for Cullen to get out. Cullen moved with difficulty; his leg was broken. He helped MacDonald bail out and then tumbled out himself, hitting the plane's tail, breaking his leg a second time. The plane exploded seconds later. They both survived.

Watching in horror, pilot Howard Moore took command of the mission, leading the way in *Suzy Q* (named after his daughter), a plane which would become one of the most storied Liberators of World War II.

After a devastating bomb run over Wilhelmshaven, Germany, the 67th was down to just five aircraft and five crews. More died over Rouen a week later and by 18 March, the 67th had flown 17 missions at the cost of five crews and six aircraft. And just four days later, the sixth original squadron crew went down. Still the missions came.

By April, only two original 67th Liberators remained: *Suzy Q* and *Little Beaver*. Crews had reached the breaking point and responded with dangerous behavior: tossing .45 cartridges into pot-belly stoves, sneaking girls into the barracks, and determined drinking. When they thought it couldn't get worse, their sister Liberator group, the 93rd, was shifted to night operations, leaving the 44th the only B-24 group left to fly the more dangerous daylight missions.

Throughout May, the 44th flew missions over Kiel, Germany, losing six planes, including *Little Beaver*. They had one easy run over Bordeaux, bombing the locks and all making it home safely. But that was it.

Then suddenly, bombsights were removed and they started training in low-level flight. Rumors abounded but not answers. Then, in July, the three 8th AAF Liberator bomb groups (44th, 93rd, and 389th) were dispatched to Africa, where they flew the murderous Ploiesti Raid. *Suzy Q* survived Ploiesti but was finally lost on a mission over Foggia, Italy. The jinx was stronger than ever.

In late August, the three groups returned to England, struck airfields in the Netherlands and convoys in the North Sea, then turned right around and returned to North Africa again, where they supported Operation Avalanche at Salerno, Italy.

In October, they hit the Austrian airplane works again, this time from the south, losing eight Liberators on the mission and another eight that crashed on the return.

So devastated was the 44th that the Air Transport Command had to be called in to transport the men back to England; they had no flyable planes left.

As new Liberator groups arrived in England in the fall of 1943, the Flying Eight Balls continued to pour it on in newly-arrived Liberators. During "Big Week" in late February 1944, they took part in raids against the German aircraft industry, hitting airfields, railroads, and V-weapon sites in preparation for the Normandy invasion in June, which they supported by attacking strong points on the beachheads.

They aided in the Saint-Lo breakthrough in July and dropped food and ammo to troops in Operation Market Garden in September, blasted the German offensive in the Battle of the Bulge in December by hitting bridges and railways, and flew resupply missions during the assault across the Rhine in March 1945.

When it was over, the 44th BG had flown a total of 343 missions, its gunners credited with 330 enemy fighters. But it lost 153 planes, the most of any B-24 group in the 8th.

ABOVE Emblem of the 44th Bomb Group, the "Flying Eight Balls."

ABOVE Officers of a 67th Squadron crew watch as the armaments crew prepares ordnance for the next mission. The apparently indestructible *Suzy Q* awaits rudder repairs in the background.

ONE DAMNED ISLAND AFTER ANOTHER

THE HAWAIIAN AIR FORCE was virtually wiped out at Pearl Harbor. It was quickly redesignated as the 7th Air Force and deployed to the Gilbert Islands, 2,000 miles southwest of Hawaii. From there, the 7th never stopped moving: 600 miles northwest to the Marshall Islands, then 900 miles west to the Carolines, then 600 miles northwest to the Marianas, 600 more miles north to Iwo Jima, and finally 1,000 miles west to Okinawa. Though it was the smallest of all the American air forces, it was tasked with conquering the largest area: 15 million square miles.

When Major General Clarence Tinker's LB-30 disappeared during the Battle of Midway, General Willis Hale took over the 7th AAF. He had his work cut out for him because the 7th always felt like second-class citizens, shared between MacArthur, Nimitz, and whoever else needed a dirty job done. Though several bomb groups came and went (the 5th Bomber Barons and the 307th Long Rangers, to name just two), the 7th finished the war with three Liberator groups: the 11th "Grey Geese," the 30th "Atoll Busters," and the last Liberator bomber group to be activated in WWII, the 494th "Kelley's Kobras."

In its first major mission, the 7th was assigned to keep the enemy's head down while Tarawa was taken. With the Navy, they pounded the atoll until it looked like it had been "dropped from 20,000 feet," and yet D-Day was a bloodbath on both sides. 2,600 Japanese soldiers were killed (only 3 surrendered) and America lost 1,500 Marines. It was a hard lesson for Admiral Nimitz: whatever level of pre-invasion bombardment you think it will take, double it. Then double it again.

In that operation, the 7th lost 7 Liberators. A month later, in January 1944, it participated in Operation Flintlock, the seventy-day pre-invasion bombardment of Kwajalein, the largest atoll in the world, in the Marshall Islands. Returning from a mission badly damaged, *Belle of Texas* of the 30th BG landed at Tarawa with no brakes, deploying three parachutes to slow her down. She stopped fifteen feet from the water's edge. But Flintlock cost the 7th another 18 Liberators.

From there, the 7th hit Eniwetok during Operation Catchpole, Wake, Jaluit in the Marshalls, Tinian and Saipan in the Marianas, and Truk, Ponape, and Kusiae in the Carolines. Every mission was at least 8 hours, often at night, always over water, with only a compass and a sextant to find their way home.

The 7th was now on Kwajalein, 1,000 miles from Truk Atoll, formerly a key naval base in the central Pacific for the Japanese, but they heard footsteps and moved to the Palaus, 1,200 miles further west. Though it was still formidable, taking Truk became pointless; the same result could be achieved by neutralizing and isolating the once-busy atoll.

The 7th was given the duty and one night in April 1944, Woodrow Waterous, pilot of *A-Vailable* of the 30th BG, was over the atoll when searchlights and flak found them as he completed his bomb run and headed out to sea. Chased by fighters, they took five cannon hits, one exploding above the co-pilot's seat, killing him and blinding Waterous. The navigator was hit in the leg. The top gunner hit the Zero and sent him flaming into the sea. The hits had destroyed the trim tab controls and much of the nose. The radio was dead and the automatic pilot as well. Waterous was dazed and bleeding and could only see blurs, but could not leave his seat. His flight engineer, Sgt. Paul Regusa, got into the co-pilot's seat and read off the instruments to Waterous.

They were five hours from base with a blind pilot and an unconscious navigator. Lt. Bob Irizarry, the bombardier, took Regusa's place and Regusa went aft into the bomb bay, where a single 500-pound bomb was dangling from its rack. Regusa and another crewman cranked the bomb bay doors open and struggled to dislodge the bomb. It came loose, then caught again halfway out of the aircraft. Now more dangerous than ever, they could not leave it there, so they struggled to get it back inside and closed the bomb bay doors.

Daylight came. All Irizarry could see was ocean. Waterous decided they'd have to ditch soon; he didn't know if they were even on the right course for Eniwetok atoll in the Marshalls.

The crew began preparing for ditching, donning Mae West vests and locating the Gibson Girl floatable radio.

And then Irizarry sighted land. It was Eniwetok. Waterous brought her in, using the eyes of his bombardier sitting beside him in the torn and bloodstained co-pilot's seat.

ATOLL BUSTERS

ABOVE Lt. Charles Pratte brings the *Belle of Texas* in safely, deploying crew parachutes.

RIGHT Emblem of the 30th Bomb Group, the "Atoll Busters."

49

BLACK SUNDAY

WHEN NAPOLEON SAID, "An army marches on its stomach," his soldiers were on foot. In modern times, armies march on gasoline, oil, and grease, and the 18- square mile refinery complex in the Danube Valley at Ploiesti, Romania, provided 30% of Hitler's fuel and oil. Unfortunately for the Allies, Ploiesti was well out of harm's way, 1,000 miles from the closest bomber bases in North Africa.

No matter, we would find a way. A trial run by Liberators from Egypt in June 1942 did little damage, but proved it was feasible. In April 1943, a daylight raid was planned, flying at low level to ensure success.

Three bomb groups from England joined the 98th Pyramiders and the 376th Liberandos, and on 1 August 1943, 200 B-24Ds took off from Benghazi, Libya, and headed across the Mediterranean. Each aircraft had 4,000 lbs of bombs and an extra fuel tank in the bomb bay, and cases of incendiary bombs that could be hand-thrown were lashed by the waist windows.

Col. Keith Compton of the Liberandos led the mission, followed by the Traveling Circus (93rd BG). The battered, older Pyramider B-24Ds soon fell behind and the Flying Eight Balls (44th BG) and Sky Scorpions (389th BG) were delayed getting off the ground. Soon the five bomb groups were stretched out along a route that would pass over the highlands of Albania and Yugoslavia before entering Romania.

At the Pindus Mountains in Albania, Compton climbed over towering cumulus clouds to summit the 9,000' peaks. By the time he entered Romania, only the Flying Circus was still with the Liberandos. As the verdant Danube valley opened up before them, Compton dove and leveled off at fifty feet, streaking toward Ploiesti.

When Compton reached the first checkpoint, he could see only a few dozen aircraft behind him. Halfway to the second checkpoint, he made a key navigation error, following a rail line not *east* to Ploiesti, but *south* to Bucharest, the best-defended city in eastern Europe. Though pilots in following aircraft broke radio silence, shouting, "Wrong turn!" they too banked and followed Compton into the maw of Bucharest's 88-mm guns. After initially getting hammered, the Flying Circus turned toward Ploiesti, leaving the Liberandos to figure out their error.

The three following groups, unaware of Compton's wrong turn, passed the second checkpoint as planned and turned on the final leg toward Ploiesti, beginning their bomb runs on refinery targets known as Red I, White I-V, and Blue I.

Within minutes, the sky over Ploiesti was smoky black as the Liberators, coming in from the north and the south, hit their targets. As the Pyramiders followed a rail line into Ploiesti, a flak gun disguised as a train opened up on them. From their fifty foot altitude, their gunners made quick work of it.

The Liberandos, arriving from the south, found it difficult to locate their assigned targets, which were shrouded in smoke, so Compton released his men to bomb "targets of opportunity." Soon, all of Ploiesti was a raging firestorm. Liberators flew so low on their bomb runs that gunners had to aim up at anti-aircraft crews on rooftops.

In the last attack of the day, the Sky Scorpions bombed Red I at Campina, twenty miles north of Ploiesti. *Old Kickapoo*, flying at just 30 feet, trailed leaking fuel which was set afire by flames rising from a previous bomb explosion. The pilot managed to maintain course for the bombing run but crash-landed in a river bed. Though four men survived the crash, two died of injuries and two gunners were captured.

Given the amount of smoke, the raid was at first thought to be a success, but the cost was devastating: 53 of 178 Liberators that made the run were lost. Only 88 returned to Libya, of which 55 had battle damage. Over 300 crewmen were killed, 108 were captured, and 78 were interned in Turkey. Though Allied intelligence estimated a loss of refining capacity of 40%, within weeks most of the damage had been repaired and by September, the net output of Ploiesti was greater than before the raid.

Operation Tidal Wave was considered a strategic failure. But they would go back again.

LEFT Emblem of the 98th Bomb Group, the "Pyramiders."

ABOVE In what is inarguably the most famous bomber photo of WWII, *The Sandman* clears the roiling smoke over the Astra- Romana refinery. The photo was taken from the tail of *Chug-a-Lug*.

UNDER THE RADAR

HEROES, ALL

NEITHER THE 5th nor the 13th Army Air Force had an auspicious beginning. On 8 December 1941, the Far East Air Force (FEAF) had just 17 B-17s on Luzon Island in the Philippines. After the Japanese attack, only two ever flew again. Stunned, the FEAF retreated to Australia, licking its wounds. But just a month later, three LB-30s (carved out of the RAF order) and two Forts carried out the first American-crewed Liberator action of the war, raiding Japanese shipping and airfields from Java.

In Australia, the FEAF was redesignated the 5th Army Air Force which, though its operational Liberators rarely exceeded 20 at any given time during the first year, harassed Japanese shipping and convoys intent on subjugating the oil-rich Dutch East Indies. About this time General "Hap" Arnold canceled all B-17 orders; only the Liberator was capable of spanning the vast watery expanses of the Pacific.

It wasn't until September 1942 that the 5th started humming with what became four of the most famous Liberator bomb groups of the war: the 22nd Red Raiders, the 43rd Ken's Men, the 380th Flying Circus, and the 90th Jolly Rogers, which was the first Liberator group to reach the southwest Pacific and which ended the war with an unequalled record, as well as boasting the most famous group emblem.

The 5th's first job was to secure Australia, then save New Guinea, blockade the Japanese at Rabaul on New Britain, subdue the Palaus, push through the Philippines, quiet Formosa, crush Okinawa, and finally whip Japan in an area three times the size of the European theater—and do it with a fraction of the planes.

But they weren't in it alone. The tiny 13th AAF, activated in November 1942, was a dozen widely-scattered units across the south central Pacific staging out of more than 40 islands—hence its nickname, the "Jungle Air Force." The 13th's two heavy bomb groups, the 307th Long Rangers and the 5th Bomber Barons, aided amphibious landings in the Gilbert, Marshall, Mariana, Palau, and Philippine islands.

A hush-hush "snooper" squadron of jet-black Liberators flew nightly missions against the "Tokyo Express" racing down "The Slot" in the Solomons, sinking as many ships at night as everyone else got during the day.

ON 26 OCTOBER 1943, Fred Hinze, flying *Golden Gator* for the Circus, had just completed his bomb run against ships in the Pomelaa harbor in the southeast Celebes, north of Australia. Things had already gone wrong with a crash on take-off and only four Liberators reaching the target. They were about to get worse.

As it came off target, an engine on *Golden Gator* was hit, setting the wing ablaze. Hinze climbed into the clouds while his crew doused the fire. When he emerged from the clouds, ten fighters jumped him and for the next forty minutes Hinze fought for his life. *Gator's* gunners got eight fighters and others were trailing smoke when they gave up.

By now, the *Gator* had lost another engine and a third was running rough. Hinze put her into a dive to windmill the balky engine back into form. As he broke through the clouds over an island and pulled out of the dive, he clipped a tree top, wedging it into the stabilizer where it remained for the rest of the flight.

He was a long way from home, so as he skirted Timor, he had the crew toss out all the guns and ammo except for 25 rounds for the top turret. For 350 miles Hinze coaxed the ship along. He knew Darwin was out of reach so he set course for Moa Island instead.

Over Moa, two Nick fighters popped up. One burst and the top gunner's ammo was gone and the ship was unarmed. The fighters came in again and again, riddling the *Gator* with holes. Suddenly the top turret exploded, killing the gunner. Another crewman headed back to get his chute and was cut in half. The nose gunner was killed when the generator he was crawling past exploded. He died in the arms of gunner Howard Collet, who pulled a Bible from his pocket and started reading it over the intercom. After just a few verses, a bullet to the stomach silenced him. The tail gunner was killed by a 20-mm shell as he hunched behind his empty guns.

The bombardier was crouched between Hinze and the co-pilot. A cannon shell exploded, shearing away the left side of Hinze's face; another removed his left foot above the ankle. His co-pilot was hit in both legs and his yoke disappeared. The bombardier applied a tourniquet to Hinze's leg while the pilot used his other foot on the rudder pedals. As a fighter zipped by without firing, Hinze joked sardonically, "Dry run."

They were going in, so the bombardier turned to open the upper hatch. Hinze was hit again in the chest, but he still got the *Gator* down onto the water. Hundreds of holes in the fuselage sunk the plane in minutes and the life rafts did not deploy. Five men escaped the sinking plane, but one went back to help another and was never seen again.

The 5th and the 13th ended up on Ie Shima and Okinawa, respectively, flying missions over Kyushu (the southernmost Japanese home island), Formosa, and Indochina. They had come a long way and were ready to go further when the atom bombs ended the war.

ABOVE Liberator B-24M s/n 44-40721 of the 5th AAF, 90th BG, 400th BS on its hardstand at Port Moresby, New Guinea, 1944.

RIGHT The emblem of the 380th Bomb Group, "The Flying Circus."

51

SEA-LEVEL SCOURGE

WHILE THEIR ARMY PEERS flew runs over Europe at 25,000' and at 15,000' over the Pacific, the Navy (who called their Liberators PB4Ys*) came in at tree-top level. Though their primary mission was long-range patrol and reconnaissance, they fully lived up to the bomber part of the aircraft's name as well.

The Navy had a score of Liberator squadrons scattered around the Pacific, often sharing a base with their Army siblings. Dispensing with heavy turbochargers and belly turrets, the deep blue-painted Libs didn't arrive until January 1943, but then went straight to work in the Solomon Islands northeast of Australia, strafing shipping convoys and carpet-bombing enemy airstrips. Early squadrons, VB-101 and 102, racked up a record that put the Army to shame. But at 500', hitting the target was easy; it was equally easy for the enemy to hit you. Losses were harrowing.

The most famous unit, VB-104, "Sear's Buccaneers," led by Lt. Harry Sears from their base on Guadalcanal, got two Presidential Unit Citations for their work, flying 9-15 hour missions every other day, their specialty being Japanese Betty bombers.

Between Guadalcanal in early 1943 and the Philippines in late 1944, Navy Libs flew in every island-hopping campaign. Their pre-invasion photo reconnaissance was invaluable and while the developed photos were still drying, they were pounding the enemy during the landing itself.

CONSOLIDATED COWBOYS

TRUK WAS A 1,200-square mile atoll in the Carolines with hull-skinning reefs, deep anchorages, seaplane bases, command centers, airfields, and scores of anti-aircraft emplacements. For good reason it was known as the "Gibraltar of the Pacific."

"Bus" Miller was a legend and so was his plane, *Thunder Mug*. On 4 April 1944, Miller was looking for a Japanese carrier in the Hall Islands, 75 miles north of Truk, but couldn't find it. Banking sharply, Miller spoke to his bow gunner: "Keep an eye open for reefs. We're going into Truk." Entering the lagoon at sea level, Miller bombed a destroyer at anchor in the first attack on Truk by a lone aircraft.

In early April, Miller single-handedly destroyed the enemy at Poluwat, an atoll 180 miles west of Truk. For the next six weeks he waged a private war against the atoll.

By mid-May, all that was left was a battered lighthouse and a radio station. Miller was lined up on the station when a three-inch shell from a flak gun atop the lighthouse exploded above the cockpit, kicking the blocks from under the top turret and pointing the barrels down. The dazed gunner kept firing and .50-caliber bullets tore through the cockpit roof, disintegrating the instrument panel and wounding Miller and his copilot.

Though he was bleeding from dozens of wounds, over the next seven hours Miller flew 850 miles, landing safely at Eniwetok in the Marshall Islands.

ABOVE Capt. Norman "Bus" Miller, commander of the VB-109 Squadron. BELOW Emblem of the VB-109 "Pirates."

ABOVE A Liberator with the distinctive round ERCO nose turret unloads on a fighter airstrip on Eten Island, Truk atoll. As usual, the P&W R-1830 engines are leaking oil.

* "PB" for Patrol Bomber, "4" for the Navy's fourth such model, and "Y" for Consolidated Aircraft. Later models with the tall, single tail appended a "-2" to the name.

CUMULO-GRANITE

IN 1937, FORMER Army Air Force officer Claire Chennault, while training Chinese pilots in Kunming, China, recruited another 300 U.S. pilots, starting the American Volunteer Group, which became known as the "Flying Tigers." Chennault persuaded FDR to approve his plan to send bombers and crews to China for use against Japan, should war come. The plan never played out because Japan struck first. In early 1942, they pushed the British out of Burma, cutting off the 700-mile Burma Road, which had kept the Nationalist Chinese supplied in their fight against the Japanese.

In April 1942, India-based 10th Air Force C-47s began a fuel airlift over the Himalayas to supply the Chinese Nationalist Army. The 500-mile route passed over the rugged Eastern Himalaya Uplift, soon dubbed "The Hump" by the pilots.

Chabua, India, was the airlift's western terminus. Chabua is just 90' above sea level, surrounded by 10,000 foot mountain walls. An eastward flight crosses a half dozen river valleys separated by 15,000' peaks. Explosive weather is the norm as moist warm air masses from the Indian Ocean produce high pressure sweeping north, which meets cold dry air from Siberia moving south, colliding to produce hail, sleet, and torrential thunderstorms. To make matters worse, in 1942 there were few reliable charts and no radio navigation aids or weather information. The pilots aptly called this collection of the world's tallest peaks "cumulo-granite."

By January 1943 the 7th Bomb Group of the 10th AAF was finally at full strength. Its Liberators bombed Japanese forces throughout Burma, but its C-87s (cargo versions of the B-24) flew the Hump, supplying now General Chennault's new 14th AAF in Kunming, which soon received the 308th BG, also a Liberator unit. Together, the two groups moved materiel across the southern Himalaya flank, mountains that played such a big part in the airmen's lives that one particular plane, *Doodlebug*, had 120 tiny snow-capped peaks stenciled on its fuselage along with 11 mission symbols and 10 Japanese flags denoting downed enemy aircraft.

Another 308th ship, Snowball from Hell, made 35 trips over the Hump by the end of 1943, one with 10 inches of ice on wing tops, frozen ailerons, and icicles dangling from the radio antenna. It landed safely in China with two engines out on one wing.

As 1943 ended, the air war in Burma heated up and the 308th BG joined the 7th BG in India, hitting marshalling yards, railways, and port facilities in the Burmese capital of Rangoon. Japanese defenses were intense and many Liberators were lost.

Meanwhile, deliveries over the Hump reached the goal of 10,000 tons a month, for which FDR gave the 10th AAF a Presidential Unit Citation.

By mid-1944, the Japanese began an immense Chinese offensive, capturing several airfields in eastern China from Chennault's 14th AAF. Liberators flew missions over coastal China, Malaya, Indochina, and Thailand, helping to halt the offensive.

ON A SOLO MISSION in the South China Sea the night of 26 October 1944, Major Horace Carswell barely missed a destroyer on his first low-level pass of a Japanese convoy. On his next pass hit a large tanker twice, but flak knocked out two engines and damaged a third, crippling his hydraulics, puncturing a gas tank, and wounding his co-pilot. Carswell limped to the China shore, struggling to reach bail-out altitude. One of his crew discovered a tear in his parachute, rendering it useless, so Carswell continued on, hoping to reach a friendly base. Then the third engine failed and Carswell rang the bailout bell. Rather than save himself, he chose to stay with his comrade and attempt a crash landing. They died when the plane hit a mountainside.

Carswell received the Medal of Honor.

LEFT Emblem of the 308th Bomb Group. Its motto means "When Struck, I Rise Again."

ABOVE B-24D Doodlebug (41-24223) with a newly-clad beauty on the nose, along with a close approximation of the name in Chinese characters.

PERCUSSUS RESURGO

TOURNIQUET

THE NORTH AFRICA campaign wrapped up in May 1943, leaving the 12th AAF with little to do while the 8th AAF in England was overwhelmed with targets. General "Hap" Arnold proposed splitting the 12th in Tunisia in two, moving half to England and, using the experienced 98th Pyramiders and the 376th Liberandos as a backbone, creating a new air force at Foggia on the ankle of the Italian peninsula. The new 15th AAF would have an unprecedented fifteen heavy bomb groups of Liberators and Fortresses. Their objective: deny the Axis fuel, oil, and aircraft.

But first, Italy would have to be secured. In July, Sicily was invaded and by September the Allies were in Italy, moving north. In December, General Jimmy Doolittle, commander of the new 15th AAF, set up his HQ. Though half of all Axis oil refineries were within 600 miles of Foggia, his air force got their start supporting the landings at Anzio, south of Rome, on Italy's western coast.

In February 1944, Doolittle's boys finally got to their mission, hitting German fighter production plants during Operation Argument, part of the "Big Week" missions, and in April, the Pyramiders and Liberandos returned to Ploiesti, Romania, this time in high-level raids, for pay-back for the abortive 1 August 1943 raid. Soon they were hitting Ploiesti regularly, along with refineries in Austria, Yugoslavia, and Hungary, taking most of the targets as the 8th AAF prepared for the French D-Day landings in June.

The Oil Campaign began with regular missions of 500-700 heavies hitting oil and factory installations all across southern Europe. The Germans at Ploiesti fought back with fighters, flak guns, and smoke pots, which they ignited when the bombers showed up on radar. By the time the planes arrived, the sky over the target would be an opaque blanket, making visual bombing impossible. The Allies, in turn, began using the new H2X "Mickey" X-band ground-mapping radar installed in place of the ball turret on "Pathfinder" Libs and Forts.

As ground forces occupied Rome in July, the 15th began softening up French targets preparatory for Operation Anvil, the invasion of southern France. They also continued hitting Austrian aircraft factories, French railways, German jet aircraft installations, and Polish synthetic oil plants, but they always returned to Ploiesti, draining away precious (and increasingly rare) Axis fuel. But Allied bomber crew losses were staggering and scores of Foggia bunks were empty after each mission.

Lt. Bernard Ball flew B-24s in the 717th BS of the 449th "Flying Horseman" bomb group. On a mission to Yugoslavia in August, an 88-mm shell struck his ship, destroying the roof over the waist windows, killing both gunners and severing the rudder and elevator cables. Ball got her home by using engine power to control pitch and yaw. (See photo, right.)

By the end of August, Ploiesti was finally finished. Though it was still producing, it was completely cut off; the 15th had destroyed local railways and mined the nearby Danube River channel. The Red Army was approaching. For the first time, post-mission reconnaissance photos showed no repair crews.

By the end of September, only three of ninety Axis oil installations were operating. Shifting focus, the 15th then hit aircraft factories in Blechhammer and Florisdorf, Austria, and Odertal, Germany. In early 1945, it even pounded targets for the Russians on the Eastern Front. It was almost over for the Axis.

Napoleon was right: starve an army and win the war.

BACKGROUND Reconnaissance photo of the Columbia Aquila oil refinery in Ploiesti, Romania.

RIGHT A German artillery soldier displays an 88-mm shell.

FORGOTTEN BATTLE

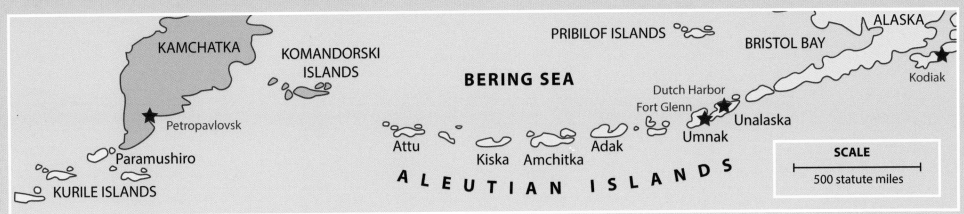

THE DOOLITTLE RAID awoke Japan to the possibility of invasion. The fact that the closest American outpost was on frozen, barren Attu Island at the western tip of the Aleutian Islands 800 miles from the Japanese Kurile Islands offered little comfort. So when Admiral Isoroku Yamamoto planned the Midway attack, the price he paid for Imperial Japanese Army involvement was an invasion of the Aleutians.

America had broken the Japanese naval code and the 11th AAF spotted the fleet on 2 June 1942. Bad weather prevented an attack and the next day the Japanese launched planes against Dutch Harbor on Unalaska Island. Met by flak and fighters, they dropped their bombs and escaped. Their second sortie the next day destroyed oil storage tanks, a hospital, and a beached ship.

Following the Dutch Harbor attack, the Japanese intended to land 1,200 men at Adak, but bad weather fouled the plan. Instead, on 6 June, they invaded Kiska and the next day, Attu, with little resistance. In retaliation, Liberators hit Kiska Harbor but were damaged by flak.

The weather downed aircraft on both sides. Between June and October the 11th AAF lost 72 planes—only 9 of them to combat. By August, the Army established a base at Adak, again hitting Kiska, and in September, a dozen Liberators of the 404th BS, late of North Africa, joined in. Known as the "Pink Elephants" for their desert sand paint scheme, they patrolled the Bering Sea.

In January 1943, the Allies invaded Amchitka, eighty miles from Kiska, and began construction of an airfield, yet only 10 tons of bombs were dropped the entire month and four Liberators were lost, none to combat, all from weather.

In May, the Allies invaded Attu in a horrific battle resulting in 4,000 American casualties and 2,300 Japanese dead in a final, bloody *banzai* charge. An airstrip was built on Attu and plans were laid for a 1944 invasion of the Kuriles.

In July, six Liberators left Attu, headed for Paramushiru Island in the Kuriles, just south of the Soviet Union's Kamchatka Peninsula. Four transports were spotted and the B-24s headed for them. Lt. Lucian Wernick's B-24 sustained nose wheel damage. Inspection revealed no hydraulics and shredded life rafts. Wernick's crew never carried life preservers—death came in ten minutes in the icy waters below. Wernick mentally reviewed the landing strip at Attu: the runway began at the water's edge and ended at the foot of a mountain. And he had no brakes.

The crew hand-cranked the main gear and gathered at the waist. Wernick landed in a near-stall, the rudders almost skidding on the ground as the mains skidded on the slippery Marston Mat. The crew began slowly walking toward the tail as the aircraft roared across the strip, keeping the nose up, aided by Wernick on elevator. As the ship rapidly approached the runway end, the entire crew save Wernick were bunched into the tail. They stopped within a few feet of the mountain and the smashed nose clunked to the ground.

In August 1943, Allied troops invaded Kiska, only to discover the Japanese had withdrawn two weeks before.

The invasion of Kuriles in northern Japan never happened, though the 11th AAF tied up several hundred planes and 40,000 Japanese troops who had been deployed there against the invasion threat. The official history of the 11th AAF states they were "at least a considerable nuisance value."

ABOVE Liberators from the 404th Bomb Squadron raid Paramushiru Island, Japan, on 18 August 1943.

TIP OF THE SPEAR

THE 8TH AIR FORCE was busy in the weeks leading up to Operation Overlord, the invasion of France. They were ordered to ground the Luftwaffe, destroy enemy communication and transportation, and on D-Day itself, strike selected targets in Pas-de-Calais as a feint to draw Germans away from Normandy, 180 miles to the south.

During May 1944, Liberators hit marshaling yards in Belgium, sent 900 bombers to Berlin, and plastered the synthetic oil plant at Politz, near Berlin. The French coast was eerily quiet, something the Germans would have noticed had they not been so busy putting out fires hundreds of miles away.

The honor of leading the invasion went to the 336th Bomb Group based at Bungay in eastern England. At 2:00 am on 6 June 1944, 450 pilots got their orders: they would hit targets in waves of three six-plane flights, with a radar-equipped ship in every third flight. No short bombing; troops would be within 400 yards of targets.

By dawn, clouds had rolled in, making radar bombing the order of what truly *was* the "longest day" as 8th AAF crews flew up to four missions each. Astonishingly, only three planes were lost: one to enemy fire and two in a mid-air collision. As Eisenhower predicted, the Luftwaffe was nowhere to be found.

But the weeks following the landing were as rough as the 8th had ever seen. In July, a lead bombardier mistakenly dropped his bombs onto American positions and the twelve ships behind him did the same. Minutes later, another bombardier mistook gun flashes for smoke markers and eleven more B-24s added their bombs to the deadly error.

The Luftwaffe singled the 492nd BG out for particular punishment: within weeks the fledgling group had the worst mission-loss ratio in the entire Army Air Forces. When it was deactivated in August, the incoming group refused to use its tail markings.

In September, Liberators supported Operation Market Garden, dropping supplies for the troops at low level and braving hellish German ground fire.

Days later, the 445th BG experienced the worst bloodbath of any single 8th AAF group: they were flying over solid cloud in central Germany and were led astray when the navigator made the wrong turn at the Initial Point. Separated from the main force, they were immediately jumped by scores of FW-190s, which shot down 25 B-24s before the P-51 Mustangs arrived to chase the attackers away.

For eleven days at the turn of the year, every 8th AAF aircraft (including assembly ships) was in the sky, destroying every German airfield within 100 miles of surrounded American GIs in the Battle of the Bulge.

But there were also milk runs and satisfying sorties: The heavies of the 8th delivered 2 million gallons of fuel to Patton's thirsty Third Army, and food and supplies to American forces moving faster across France than their supply trains.

But even as the number of Luftwaffe fighters dwindled, their tactics grew ever bolder. On 7 April 1945, a *Sonderkommando Elbe* Me-109 purposely slammed into a B-24, disintegrating the cockpit. It rolled onto its back and took another bomber with it to the ground. That day there were eight victims of these unprecedented German-style *kamikaze* attacks. Strangely, it was too much even for the Luftwaffe: the bloody tactic was not seen again in European skies.

LEFT Emblem of the 8th Army Air Force, the "Mighty Eighth."

CENTER B-24H Liberators of the 446th Bomb Group sortie on D-Day, 6 June 1944.
BACKGROUND LSTs line up at Utah Beach, 6 June 1944.

ON THE DOORSTEP

OPERATION ICEBERG, the 1 April 1945 invasion of Okinawa, was as big as Normandy and just as costly. 180,000 men, brought in on 1,200 ships, battled an estimated 100,000 Japanese soldiers and 20,000 Okinawan militia. As had become the norm, there was little resistance on the beaches, but inland all hell broke loose. And at sea, almost 1,500 kamikazes sunk 38 ships and damaged 368.

From thousands of bunkers throughout the island, the Japanese fought to the death; Allied troops had to clear them, cave by cave, with flamethrowers. Civilians were used as human shields and bombs. Night infiltrations resulted in brutal hand-to-hand combat. Then the monsoons hit, turning the island into a sea of sticky mud. As days stretched into weeks, soldiers and Marines hunkered down in foxholes full of water, feces, and dead bodies; the battlefield became a combination latrine, garbage dump, and graveyard. Before the island was secured after 83 numbing days, 75,000 Japanese soldiers and 150,000 Okinawan civilians were dead as well as 14,000 American soldiers and Marines.

But it was a prerequisite for Operation Downfall, the invasion of Japan scheduled for 1 November. As areas became secure, construction battalions (CBs or SeaBees) got to work building eighteen runways on Okinawa for bombers and three on Ie Shima for fighter escorts. Kadena and Yontan airfields were soon up and running and on 24 June, the Liberators of the 494th Kelley's Kobra's were the first to touch down, with Ken's Men, Jolly Rogers, and Flying Circus of the 5th AAF to follow shortly.*

Kyushu Island, the southernmost Japanese home island, is just 350 miles north of Okinawa. On 5 July, 48 B-24s from the 494th got into the air in a record 48 minutes, striking Omura Airfield on Kyushu, achieving a 50% hit rate and becoming the first bomb group to hit a target on the enemy mainland from Okinawa.

The battleship *Haruna* was a veteran of almost every naval battle of the Pacific and she was moored at Kure Harbor near Hiroshima. The Army and the Navy had a friendly wager as to who would get her first, and Col. Kelley of the 494th wanted the prize.

So, on 28 July 1945, his bombers faced a near-opaque curtain of flak over the harbor. *Lonesome Lady*, piloted by Lt. Tom Cartwright, was hit, her hydraulics gushed fluid, and Cartwright had no choice. He rang the bail-out bell and everyone hit the silk.

He landed in a pine forest and surrendered to a farmer, who took him to a police station where he saw his co-pilot. They were blindfolded and placed in the town square where they were pinched and struck all night by furious civilians. The next morning, they were taken by truck to a prison where they saw the rest of his crew, except two.

Cartwright was interrogated, mostly about why Hiroshima had been spared bombing. He had no idea but they did not believe him. He was separated from his crew, bound and blindfolded again, and placed on a train that chugged north for two days. Cartwright began to feel sorry for himself, separated from his comrades. At a Tokyo military base, he was interrogated for three days, the questioning always starting out friendly and gradually turning angrier, with threats of punishment if he did not cooperate. They questioned him particularly closely about a new, powerful bomb, of which he of course knew nothing.

Shortly after the last interrogation, he was blindfolded, taken outside and forced to kneel, his head pressed against a wooden block. There were shouts and angry voices. He could feel their sizzling hatred and an intense desire for vengeance against him personally. He was certain he was about to be beheaded.

Then suddenly he was jerked to his feet and led back to his cell. A few days later, he was told the war was over. When he inquired about his crew, he was informed that the prison where they had been held was just a half-mile from the epicenter of the explosion of the atomic bomb over Hiroshima.

CENTER As a Higgins boat approaches Omuri Island in Tokyo Bay, Allied prisoners of war cheer ecstatically, including Lt. Tom Cartwright of the 7th Air Force, third from right.

* With the war in Europe over, the 8th AAF was scheduled to join them, but never had to make the trip. The B-29 Superfortresses of the 20th AAF were already in the Marianas, nightly firebombing Tokyo.

57

FAMOUS CREWMEN

BIERNE LAY pilot 8/490

The co-writer of *Twelve O'clock High* flew both B-17s on the costly 17 August 1943 Schweinfurt-Regensburg mission and commanded the 490th BG, which flew Liberators. Shot down over France following D-Day, the Resistance helped him rejoin Allied advance units.

LOUIS ZAMPERINI bombardier 13/307/372

Made famous by the book *Unbroken*, Louis's life reads like a script: juvenile delinquent, Olympic athlete, Wake Island attack survivor, castaway (47 days), and POW. Alcoholism nearly ruined his life after the war but a conversion to Christianity saved him and helped him forgive his tormentors.

GEORGE McGOVERN pilot 15/455/741

McGovern flew 35 missions from San Giovanni, Italy, in his plane *Dakota Queen*, named in honor of his wife Eleanor. He received the Distinguished Flying Cross for safely landing on a fighter strip, saving his crew. On his last mission, his plane sustained 110 flak holes. He became a U.S. Senator from South Dakota.

JOSEPH McCONNELL navigator 8/448

Disqualified as a pilot, McConnell was trained as a navigator, flying sixty combat missions in Europe. He learned to fly after the war and flew the F-86 Sabre in Korea, shooting down sixteen MiG-15s. He was the first American triple jet-on-jet ace. Received the DSC, the Silver Star, and the DFC.

JOSEPH KENNEDY PB4Y pilot Navy/110/SAU 1

After completing 25 anti-sub missions, Kennedy volunteered for Operation Aphrodite, which crashed explosive-laden B-24 drones into enemy targets. Kennedy and his co-pilot flew a drone into the air, armed the explosive, and were supposed to bail out. The aircraft exploded, killing them both.

JIMMY STEWART pilot 8/453

He fought for the right to fight. They wanted him safe but he wanted to serve and ended up leading a squadron, then a group, flying as command pilot in the lead B-24 on dozens of missions. He received two Distinguished Flying Crosses, the Croix de Guerre, and Air Medal with three oak leaf clusters.

CREWMEN WHO *SHOULD* BE FAMOUS

WALTER STEWART   pilot   8/93/

Stewart flew 32 missions, his second to last just behind the group leader on the famous 1 August 1943 Ploiesti mission in his Liberator, *Utah Man*, which sustained heavy damage on the run. Stewart earned the Medal of Honor and the Silver Star and served thirty years in the Utah National Guard.

SAMUEL NEELEY   pilot   9/98/344

Flying his plane *Raunchy*, 1st Lt. Neeley was shot down as he approached target at tree-top level on the 1 August 1943 Ploiesti, Romania, raid. It crashed into flames, killing eight men, including Neeley, but two survived and were taken captive. He posthumously received the DFC.

BEN KUROKI   top turret gunner   8/93/409

Kuroki first flew thirty missions (including the low-level Ploiesti raid) over Europe when only 25 were required, then became the first Japanese-American to fly in combat in the Pacific, flying another 28 missions in a B-29 over mainland Japan. Recipient of the DFC and Air Medal with five oak clusters.

SABU DASTAGIR   tail gunner   13/307/370

A famous Indian child actor, Sabu (as he was known), became an American citizen in 1944 and immediately joined the USAAF, flying several dozen missions in *Flying Boxcar* and receiving the Distinguished Flying Cross for his bravery.

ARTHUR ELDER   PB4Y pilot   Navy VPB-117

During seven weeks beginning in February 1945, "Blue Raiders" pilot Elder destroyed 26,000 tons of enemy shipping and damaged another 30,000 tons, shot down two aircraft, destroyed twelve on the ground, and raided shore installations from Sarawak to Borneo to Tourane on the Indochina coast.

OMER KEMP*   pilot   7/494/865

Never letting let his handicap be known (partial deafness), Kemp worked twice as hard, bringing his men home safely on sixteen harrowing missions over the Palaus, Truk, Philippines, and finally Japan itself. Quiet, unassuming, and competent, he led by example, both personally and professionally.

FAMOUS LIBERATORS

BLUE STREAK / TEGGIE ANN   B-24D   9/376/514*

Veteran of the first high-level Ploiesti raid, this ship went on to survive 110 missions in nineteen months and 1,058 combat hours. Its scorecard reads one destroyer, one merchant vessel, one tanker, and 23 enemy aircraft, dropping 297 tons of bombs and never losing a man.

HAIL COLUMBIA   B-24D   9/98/344

Squadron commander John "Killer" Kane's personal aircraft, which he flew on the 1 August 1943 low-level Ploiesti raid where it was hit by anti-aircraft fire, taking more than 20 hits. Kane completed the mission and crashed-landed on Cyprus. Everyone walked away from the wreckage.

COMMANDO   Liberator II   Air Ministry

British Prime Minister Winston Churchill's private aircraft, in which he flew diplomatic missions across the European Theater, including the crucial flight to Moscow for high-level talks with Stalin. Disappeared on 26 March 1945 on a flight to Canada. The PM was not on board.

SUPER MAN   B-24D   7/11/98

Made famous in the book and film *Unbroken*, this aircraft sustained 600 holes from enemy fighters and flak on a mission to bomb phosphate works on Nauru Island. Bombardier Louis Zamperini saved the day when he used bomb-arming wires to repair the rudder control cables

STRAWBERRY BITCH   B-24D   9/376/512

Flew 56 combat missions from North Africa in 1943-44 with the famed 376th Liberandos bomb group, hitting Italy, Greece, Austria, and the Ploiesti, Romania, oil refineries. Now on display at the U.S. Air Force Museum in Dayton, OH.

DIAMOND LIL / 'OL 927   B-24A/LB-30   CAC

The eighteenth B-24 built and given British s/n AM927, *Lil* was on her way to England in 1941 when a strut was damaged on landing. Back in San Diego, Consolidated used it as a transport during the war. Now operated by the Commemorative Air Force in Air Transport Command/neutrality livery.

LIBERATORS THAT *SHOULD* BE FAMOUS

HOT STUFF   B-24D   8/93/330

The first American heavy bomber to complete 25 missions (yes, before the B-17 *Memphis Belle*) was recalled to the U.S. for a War Bond tour but crashed in an instrument landing in Iceland, killing fourteen, including Lt. Gen. Frank Andrews, Commander of the European Theater of Operations.

CURLY BIRD   B-24J   7/30/819

The first American bomber to complete forty missions in the Pacific Theater. It went on to fly another twenty-five missions. Note the black underside, indicating its role in night missions.

BOLIVAR   B-24J   7/30/27

Completed 81 missions before being sent home for a War Bond tour, where it crash-landed at Vultee Air Field, CA, on 10 November 1944 and was scrapped. In its honor, another 7th AAF Liberator was christened *Bolivar Jr.*

BRIEF   B-24M   7/494/867

There is still spirited debate as to whether *brief* was hit by AA fire or bombed by another B-24 over the Palaus, fueled by amazing footage which captured the horrific moment on film. Find the video on YouTube and judge for yourself.

BOMERANG   B-24D   8/93/328

This aircraft participated in the first transatlantic formation flight and sustained 200 flak holes on its first mission, but kept flying, thus its name. It was the first 8th AAF Liberator to complete fifty missions and was a survivor of the ill-fated 1 August 1943 Ploiesti Raid.

BLACK CAT   B-24J   8/466/784

The last American bomber to be shot down in the war, it was on a mission to bomb a railway bridge in Salzburg, Austria, on 21 April 1945, when cloud cover prevented hitting the target. It was downed by flak at the secondary target. Ten crew members died, two survived as POWs.

FAMOUS NOSE ART

BREWERY WAGON   B-24D   9/376/512

A part of the low-level Ploiesti raid, Lt. John Palm did not take the wrong turn at Targoviste, but headed straight for Ploiesti, alone, taking a direct hit in the nose and getting strafed by an Me-109. His left leg shot off, he still managed to land safely southwest of Ploiesti, saving the rest of his crew.

WILLIT RUN   B-24H   8/392

A clever play on words for a problematic ship built by Ford at its Willow Run, MI, factory (a former Ford automobile plant), showing a Ford sedan with a sprung radiator and a flat font tire, obviously a commentary on the reliability of this particular aircraft.

BOURBON BOXCAR   F-7A   5/6/20

Talk about making whiskey from lemons, this crew figured that if it's a flying boxcar, then what's it carrying? In this case, they're firing whiskey bottles as they take recon photos (as all F-7As did) and perhaps mulling them over later at the Officer's Club with a golden shot of Kentucky's best.

PLAYMATE   B-24J   7/494/867

The almost 200 glamorous and tantalizing "pin-up girls" painted by Peruvian artist Alberto Vargas for *Esquire* magazine in the 1930s and 1940s were often used as nose art but never so faithfully as on this Pacific Liberator, taking many an airman's mind off war and steering it toward... *play*.

IT AINT SO FUNNY   B-24L   5/43/64

One of S/Sgt Sarkis Bartigian's most elaborate works depicts a panoply of popular cartoon characters of the time, all apparently in conflict with each other: Dick Tracy, Lil' Abner, Eddie Cantor, Wimpy, Olive Oyl, Popeye, Little Orphan Annie, Donald Duck, Batwoman, Henry, and Tarzan.

THE GOON   B-24D   14/308/374

Arthur Benko sits proudly by the top turret from which he shot down sixteen Japanese fighters. *The Goon,* named after a silent caveman Popeye comic character, had two engines out on two different missions, forcing bail outs but landed ably in both cases by its pilots in China.

62   The three numbers following the Liberator type are the air force, the bomb group, and the bomb squadron in which the aircraft flew.

NOSE ART THAT *SHOULD* BE FAMOUS

VIRGO   B-24H   8/486/834

Commercial artist Phil Brinkman (whose MOS was "draftsman") painted zodiac-themed nose art on all twelve of the 834th BS "Fighting Zodiacs" ships. His work must have been lucky; none of the squadron's ships were lost.

HANGOVER HAVEN II   F-7A   5/6/20

Artist Al Merkling was another of the greats. *Hangover* flew 39 missions as a photo ship for the 20th Combat Mapping Squadron. The color photo proves it: that's a pink elephant.

CONSOLIDATED MESS   B-24J   7/11/98

This one proves they weren't all titillating. Owing to so many crews' love-hate relationship with the Liberator, there were ten B-24s in the war called *Consolidated Mess*, but this is the best and funniest. And to rub it in, on the other side of the nose they painted the words: "Tropical Dream."

RED ASS   B-24H   8/466/704

The 466th BG led the D-Day invasion and *Red Ass* led the 466th. Some considered the name crude so it was later changed to *Bungay Buckaroo* to honor the bomb group, English base. Now on display at the Pima Air & Space Museum, AZ.

THE JOLLY ROGER EXPRESS   B-24J   5/90/400

As often as pin-ups appeared on the noses, so did Disney characters. Here we see Donald Duck in a maniacal rage chasing Japanese Prime Minister Hideki Tojo with a black mallet with the famous Jolly Roger skull-and-cross-bombs emblem on the business end.

RUGGED BUT RIGHT   B-24H   8/448/712

This proves that the shark mouth that looked so good on P-40s was also perfect for B-24s. It probably scared a few Me-109s away, and along with its crews' prowess, helped it survive the war, only to succumb to the guillotine chopper at the reclamation center in Altus, OK, in October 1945.

U.S. ARMY AIR FORCE INSIGNIA

GENERAL "HAP" ARNOLD wanted a new insignia for the Army Air Force and staff member James Rawls was frustrated. Each time he'd come up with a design, Arnold would say, "No, that's not it," giving little instruction beyond the fact that it needed to include wings.

Rawls was out of ideas. How many ways could he draw wings, anyway? Then one day he happened across a picture of Winston Churchill flashing his well-known "V for Victory" sign. Rawls made a quick sketch, bending the wings up, and Arnold said, "That's just what I wanted!"

The winged star was thereafter known as the Hap Arnold emblem.

The blue disk represents the air. The white star with the red disk had been the roundel on U.S. military airplanes since 1921.* The golden wings, of course, represent victory.

Northeast U.S.

Northwest U.S.

Southeast U.S.

Western U.S.

Australia, Southwest Pacific

Caribbean, Americas

Hawaii, Central Pacific

Europe

North Africa, Middle East

India, Burma

Alaska

North Africa, Mediterranean

South Pacific

China

Mediterranean

India, China, Marianas

* The red disk was removed from aircraft roundels in 1942 to prevent confusion with Japanese markings, called "meat balls" by the airmen.

The Airframe

AN INAUSPICIOUS START

ITS BEGINNING WAS ORDINARY. On a hot August 1944 afternoon, a silver-skinned B-24J, serial number 44-44052, smelling of solvent, new rubber, and Cosmoline, rolled off the assembly line to join several other sequentially-numbered Liberators already baking in the bright Texas sun, just one of the 4,000 built at the Consolidated Fort Worth factory in 1944. Like all the others, it had a Consolidated A-6B tail turret and an Emerson A-15 nose turret, as well as a Briggs/Sperry A-13 ball turret—all standard equipment now on the J model. By then all five production plants from California to Michigan were churning out B-24Js, one every 56 minutes at Willow Run.

But there were two things that made this B-24 special: One, it would beat the daunting one-in-three odds and survive the war. Two, out of over 19,256 B-24s built between 1940 and 1945, it would be the last bomber variant still flying 70 years later. How it survived to become the Collings Foundation's *Witchcraft* is a tale in itself.

In the grips of 1930s isolationism, Congress passed the Neutrality Acts, which prohibited America from selling arms on credit or loaning money to any belligerent nation in any conflict. But after WWII broke out, public opinion began changing. Newsreels of the Blitz horrified Americans and by late 1940 the U.K. stood alone against the Axis powers. Prime Minister Winston Churchill begged President Franklin Roosevelt to rescue his flagging nation, now on the precipice.

Roosevelt conceived of a way to help the Allies without violating the neutrality laws. The idea was to base aid on considerations of self-preservation, allowing America to supply Allied nations with food, oil, and materiel if doing so was "vital" to the defense of the United States. In return, aid recipients would grant America military bases in their countries and would return or destroy the "loaned" materiel at the cessation of hostilities. The resulting Act was called the "Lend-Lease" bill and was approved by Congress in early 1941 along party lines. Lend-Lease opened a floodgate of aid and England quickly ordered the first of what eventually totaled over 700 B-24 Liberators operated by the RAF, including 44-44052, which the RAF designated a "Liberator GR Mk. VI"* and assigned serial number KH191.

The aircraft was ferried to the South East Asia Command (SEAC) and assigned to No. 8 Squadron, based at RAF Khormaksar in Aden, Yemen, at the southern tip of the Arabian peninsula. Throughout the remainder of 1944 and into early 1945, it escorted convoys and engaged in anti-submarine patrols.

As the European war reached its conclusion in May 1945, No. 8 Squadron replaced No. 200 Squadron, a "special duties" unit which flew Liberators out of RAF Jessore in eastern India and had been engaged in dropping supplies to Allied troops in Burma and Malaya.

But within two weeks, No. 8 Squadron—now flying Liberators—was ordered to Minneriya, Ceylon, off the southeastern Indian coast. There it was used to drop supplies to guerilla forces operating in Malaya and Sumatra. Operations reached their peak in July with 54 sorties flown.

In August, Japan surrendered. No. 8 Squadron kept busy, flying food and medical supplies to area Allied POW camps.

By October, with the onset of the monsoon season, operations were suspended, and in November, No. 8 Squadron was disbanded.

Under Lend-Lease, the RAF's Liberators either had to be returned to the U.S. or destroyed. With the B-24 now eclipsed by the new B-29, made famous by destroying Hiroshima and Nagasaki, America didn't want, or need, the old bombers returned, so the RAF flew its Liberators to Chakeri Airfield near Kanpur in eastern India and disabled them (often by merely shoveling sand into the fuel tanks), certifying that they had been "destroyed" under the Act.

As of 11 April 1946, KH191 was accordingly struck "off charge" and abandoned at Chakeri Airfield, where it sat among seventy of its fellow castoffs for two long years.

Ground crews of 356 Squadron RAF based on the Cocos Islands in the southern Indian Ocean celebrate the news of Japan's surrender, a Liberator B Mk. VI in the background.

LEFT The emblem of No. 8 Squadron RAF, its Latin motto translated as "Everywhere Unbounded." The Arabian *khunjah* dagger was adopted as the unit's badge.

* The British called the B-24J the "Liberator Mk. VI." Variants included "B" for land bombers, "C" for cargo, and "GR" for General Reconnaissance.

THE PARTITIONING OF INDIA in August 1947 meant the end of the British Raj. It was also the end of the Royal Indian Air Force, which morphed into the Indian Air Force (IAF). At the same time, Pakistan was formed from western, mostly Muslim, India. It almost immediately precipitated a war with India over the unaligned Kashmir region.

Suddenly, India needed bombers but had none—only the seventy "off charge" derelict Liberators at Chakeri Airfield. IAF technicians surveyed the planes and were astonished at their relatively good condition... with a little work, these birds might fly again.

In 1957, the IAF B-24s were replaced by Martin B-57 Canberras as India's first-line bomber defense, but No. 6 Squadron continued using the Liberators as trainers. It is unclear whether KH191 was one of these, as its documentation lacks an "HE" number given to active IAF aircraft. However, as late as 1972 it was serving as a static air and ground crew trainer at the Indian Air Force Technical College in Bangalore.

By December 1968, when the B-24 was officially retired, only six of the Liberator GR Mk. VIs were still active, some airframes having accumulated 40,000 hours flying time in IAF service. Their last operational sortie for the IAF was a mercy mission on Christmas Eve of that year.

Cannibalizing the worst-off ships, the IAF made forty-two B-24s airworthy, flying them to Bangalore, where Hindustan Aeronautics, Ltd, which had maintained RAF aircraft during the war, fully restored them using only scavenged or self-fabricated parts.

Thirty-two of these restored Liberators, KH191 among them, flew with the Nos. 5, 6, and 16 Squadrons of the IAF. Some received radomes in place of their ball turrets. All engaged in Air and Sea Rescue (ASR) duty. They also were called upon to transport food, supplies, and troops all over the immense subcontinent.

During India's annexation of the Portuguese-held western Goa district in 1961, Liberators dropped surrender leaflets and in 1962's border conflict with China, they provided transport support. During the 1965 war with Pakistan, they engaged in maritime patrols. Also in 1965, IAF Liberators were the first aircraft to photograph the summit of Mt. Everest. Perhaps KH191 had the honor.

During their final years of service, several Liberators were donated or sold to museums and warbird operators in Canada, the U.K., and the U.S. By this time, it was eastern Indian airmen instructing their western counterparts in the operation of an aircraft built in America and flown by Allied forces twenty years before.

One of the No. 6 Squadron Liberators has a place of honor at the Indian Air Force Museum in New Delhi. Another, *Bungay Buckaroo* (s/n 44-44175, built soon after 44-44052 at Fort Worth), is displayed at the Pima Air and Space Museum in Tucson, AZ, with its IAF No. 6 Squadron markings still in place on the starboard side.

ABOVE RIGHT The emblem of the IAF No. 6 Squadron. The motto, in Devanagari script, is "Always Alert."

A TALE OF TWO COLLECTORS

FOR THIRTEEN YEARS, KH191 disappears from the record. Perhaps it stood guard at the Indian Air Force Training Academy in Bangalore. Perhaps it was returned to the boneyard at Kanpur, along with the remains of its fellow No. 6 Squadron members. Or perhaps it was just rotting away at some Indian airport, its tires going slowly flat, its paint oxidizing under the equatorial sun, and its Plexiglas yellowing and cracking.

All we really know is that in March 1981, Doug Arnold, owner of Warbirds of Great Britain at Blackbushe Airport in southern England, purchased the airframe. During WWII, Blackbushe was an RAF Mosquito base and Arnold collected and restored aircraft in his hangars there, including Mosquitoes and Spitfires.

Arnold, who made a fortune in flea markets, had KH191 disassembled in India, and on 6 May 1982, Heavylift Cargo Airlines of Belfast, Ireland, loaded the pieces in an immense Short "Belfast" cargo plane and the Liberator began what might have been its last flight, though not under its own power.

For a couple of years, Arnold kept his prize in a Blackbushe hangar, considering when and how he would restore the aircraft. But with too many other restoration projects in progress, he finally decided to sell it and listed the airframe in the aviation sales magazine *Trade-A-Plane*.

Several potential buyers, including the Smithsonian Air & Space Museum in Washington, D.C. and the Confederate Air Force in Texas, considered purchasing the plane but eventually determined that the restoration was not feasible for them.

A few years earlier, a young mechanical engineer named Bob Collings had organized a foundation to celebrate American history and technology. His first collection pieces were classic cars. Bob Collings had an impressive educational background, with degrees from Purdue, Indiana, and Harvard. His professional career started in 1967 when computers were just on the horizon, invisible to almost everyone except young men like him who saw their nearly unlimited potential.

While finishing his doctoral thesis, Collings went to work for Digital Equipment Corporation (DEC) at a time when Sears, Roebuck & Co. needed a cash register that was more than an adding machine, one that could store information, calculate sales tax and correct errors, and handle credit card sales. DEC bowed out of the Sears deal, so Collings formed Data Terminal Systems with a partner and together they invented the first stand-alone electronic cash register. "We just listened to what our clients wanted," he says, "and gave it to them."

Cash registers handle money and for his labors Bob earned his fair share. He had a specific use for his earnings: he would become a full-time historian fashioning hands-on living history educational experiences centered around his growing collection.

Though not a pilot, he was fascinated by anything mechanical, and that included aircraft. When his son Rob was three, the boy announced that he was going to be a Corsair pilot someday. His interest in aviation grew as he did, so in 1984, when Rob was ten and Bob read Doug Arnold's ad in *Trade-A-Plane*, Bob saw a way to help make Rob's dreams of flying come true. Soon he was on an airliner to England.

At Blackbushe, Arnold greeted Collings coolly, bragging about having owned fifty-six Rolls Royces and wavering on the deal Collings was there to strike. In addition to KH191, Arnold also had a B-17 Flying Fortress for sale and an agreement was made to purchase both aircraft.

Collings' enthusiasm for the sale may have caused Arnold to wonder if he'd made a good bargain and when Arnold tried to renege on the deal, Bob had to go to court to enforce the contract. "I had to get an injunction to prevent him from selling the plane he already sold to me to someone else," said Collings, dismayed.

Eventually Arnold completed the sale on the B-24 only and soon the Liberator's engines, fuselage, tail, wings, and spare parts were strapped to the deck of a cargo ship heading west for America. After a voyage of three weeks, the parts were loaded on four tractor trailers that took them to a hangar that Bob had specially built at his Stow, MA, museum.

Now the real work would begin.

RESTORATION

BOB COLLINGS' PLAN was to restore the aircraft for static display only. Though it was a rare find indeed, it was simply too expensive to do more. Word got out and airmen who flew the Liberator soon began inquiring about how they could help in the restoration. Though the interior was a plundered mess (see photo, center left), the exterior could be restored to static display standards with reasonable effort.

But as the men began crawling through the Liberator, they noticed what the Indian Air Force had noticed back in 1947: the airframe itself was in good condition. Soon, they began to query Bob Collings about the possibility of a complete, flyable restoration.

At first he was doubtful. Restoring the ship to static display was expensive enough, but to fly it again would cost millions of dollars. What finally convinced him was their point that flying the aircraft accomplished the Foundation's stated mission. "We were convinced by the argument that only about three thousand people a year would see a static display," said Collings, "but three million might see it on a nationwide tour" and those millions might help cover the cost of the restoration.

But a flying restoration requiring FAA-approved mechanics was too extensive for the Foundation and its volunteers to handle alone, and so the restoration of the powerplants, airframe, and systems was turned over to Tom Reilly's Vintage Aircraft of Kissimmee, FL.

PPG industries of Pittsburgh, PA, supplied nose turret glass, and United Technologies of Hartford, CT, donated a Norden bombsight.

As the 50th anniversary of the first Liberator flight approached in 1989, Convair's successor, General Dynamics, came on board as a restoration sponsor.

Meanwhile, local volunteers spent thousands of hours restoring turrets, armaments, radios, the oxygen system, and other cosmetic details.

Over 80% of the plane's 1.2 million parts received attention during the 97,000 man hours of work—half of it by volunteers.

The total restoration cost came in at $1.4 million. In June 1989, the FAA approved a new registration number N224J—a nod to the aircraft type—and in September the aircraft flew once more. Beautifully.

Back in 1989, Bob Collings intended to fly the aircraft for five years and then put it on static display. It has been such a crowd favorite that for nearly 30 years it has been on an almost non-stop nationwide tour, thrilling millions.

ABOVE RIGHT For a time, the livery feted the 8th AAF bomber *All American* on the port nose and the 15th AAF Liberator *Golden Girl* on the starboard nose with a nod to Schlitz, a restoration contributor.

ALL AMERICAN

THE SHIP WAS APTLY NAMED. Like a world-class athlete, *All American* set a record that still stands today, more than seventy years later.

In summer 1943, Lt. Robert Arbuthnot of Salina, KS, joined the 461st Bomb Group at Wendover, UT. He learned to fly the Liberator in battered B-24D models, but upon completing of their training, when he arrived at Hammer Field in California, he received a brand-new B-24G* Liberator which he named *All American*.

In February 1944, the 461st "Liberaiders" deployed to Torretta Airfield on Italy's ankle. The single airstrip was gravel, with a pronounced hump in the middle and mud pits at each end. A month after their arrival, they started going after targets in southern Europe and participated in the Oil Campaign, targeting Brux, Vienna, and Ploiesti.

On 25 July, *All American* joined 23 other Liberators in an attack on the Herman Göring Tank Works at Linz, Austria. Arbuthnot led the 765th Squadron's six aircraft flight. They arrived over target at 1100. Just after the bomb bay doors opened, they were attacked by 150 enemy aircraft which came up under the formation and fired rockets into the bomb bays. Chaos ensued, with inexperienced pilots scattering, giving the Germans even more targets as they picked off outliers. Eleven bombers went down as parachutes, tracers, rockets, enemy fighters, and exploding bombers filled the air.

All American was leading the last flight in the formation. As the enemy planes flew past, attacking the leaders, Arbuthnot's gunners had a field day, nailing fourteen aircraft with an additional six probably destroyed and three damaged. A record.

It was the first time the 461st had been turned back short of its target.

On 4 October, *All American* joined 27 other Liberators in bombing railroad marshalling yards in Munich. Flak over target was intense, accurate, and heavy, and brought down seven ships that day. *All American* was hit. Lt. Robert Chalmers (Arbuthnot's crew had rotated home) coaxed the aircraft over the Alps but was unable to make it back to Torretta. Last seen north of Trieste, Chalmers and his crew bailed out before *All American* crashed into the Alp foothills near Tolmin, Yugoslavia.

For ten days they were listed as MIA. But on 14 October, the whole crew arrived back in Torretta. Incredibly, no one was injured during the bail-out and once on the ground they were found by Yugoslav partisans who helped them get home.

The 461st became one of the war's most renowned bomb groups, dropping 13,000 tons of bombs, destroying 129 enemy aircraft, and losing 108 Liberators.

As the war ground to a close in Europe, the Liberaiders dropped supplies to POW camps in Austria and in June were advised they would be deployed to the Pacific. While they preparing for the move in Sioux Falls, SD, Japan surrendered and the Group was inactivated a month later.

CREW 39
Standing L to R: Eliza Massie (ttg), Robert Molyneux (wg),
Eric English (wg), Warren Moss (ng), Hugh Baker (ttg), Roy Walkama (btg).
Kneeling L to R: Robert Arbuthnot (p), Jack Gunn (cp), William Patterson (b), Leland Harp (n).

ABOVE The emblem of the 461st Bomb Group, the "Liberaiders," whose motto, *Al Ataque*, is Spanish for "On the Attack."

* By now all five factories were turning out B-24Js with various turrets. The "G" was made by North American Aircraft in Dallas, which provided most of the 15th AAF's Liberators.

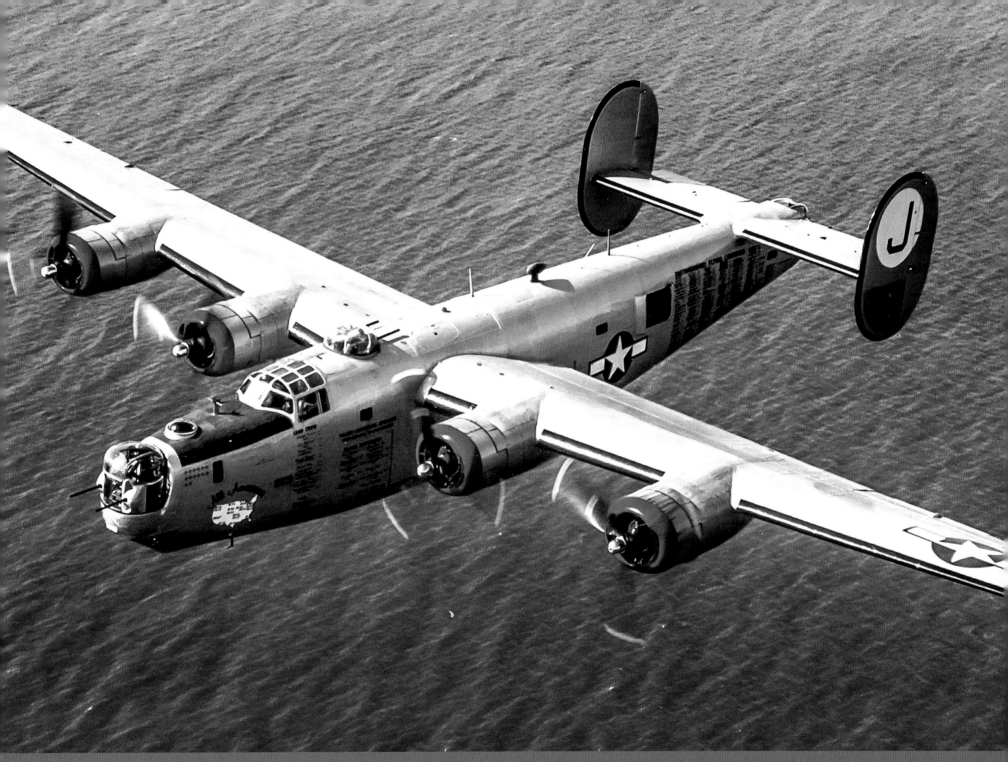

THE DRAGON AND HIS TAIL

THERE WAS NOTHING UNUSUAL about B-24J 44-40973 when it rolled off the line at the San Diego Consolidated factory in June 1944. It was the glinting, polished aluminum now preferred by the Army Air Force but sadly, like all Liberators, it was still a fat-bellied, ponderous, awkward duck. No one then would have imagined that this particular Liberator would, thanks to the brush of a talented artist, turn into a graceful swan, bearing the most famous nose (ahem, *body*) art of any aircraft of World War II.

The 380th "Flying Circus" was the second Liberator group to be assigned to the 5th AAF. From its RAAF base in Darwin, Australia, between July 1943 and late 1944, the Circus covered a million square-miles of the Dutch East Indies, providing bomber support for the New Guinea campaign, neutralizing Japanese bases, and harassing Axis shipping in the southwest Pacific.

In February 1945, the 380th moved to Mindoro Island in the Philippines. General MacArthur had landed on Leyte Island the previous October, and Luzon and Mindoro were invaded in January. The moment Mindoro was secure, an airfield was built. On 10 May 1945, 44-40973 flew a single mission for the 528th Squadron* to hit an airdrome at Tien Ho, near Canton, China.

The aircraft was then transferred to another 5th AAF group, the 43rd BG "Ken's Men," which had introduced skip-bombing, a low-level technique developed by the British "dam busters," to the Pacific. The 43rd had been based in Australia, New Guinea, Leyte, and was currently at Clark Field on Luzon Island in the Philippines.

Among many others, Bartigian painted *Cocktail Hour* and *Mabel's Labels,* which featured his smiling wife Mabel in front of several nudes strategically "labeled" with full, red lips.

When 973 arrived at Clark, everyone noticed now naked it was. It had no name or nose art, unusual for a combat Liberator. Sitting sadly unadorned on the ramp, 973 came to the attention of S/Sgt Sarkis Bartigian, who has been called the "Michelangelo of Aviation Art." Bartigian was 37, much older than most airmen. A commercial artist before the war, he spent his free time painting nose art on several 43rd BG Liberators.

The 43rd BG ended the war on the tiny island of Ie Shima off Okinawa's west coast. It was there that Bartigian got to work on 973, creating a masterpiece of aviation art that literally defies description. Fortunately, there are pictures.

In August 1945, *The Dragon and His Tail* wound up at the Kingman, AZ, reclamation plant. It was rumored to be the last Liberator to be disposed of because workers were hoping someone would appear and save it from its fate. In 1946, when it was finally shredded and smelted, a Liberator could be purchased for just $2,000.

* According to sketchy records, 973 was in the U.S. at least until November 1944. There is no record of its location after that until its first mission on 10 May 45.

WITCHCRAFT: APTLY NAMED

LIBERATOR 42-52534 came off the assembly in December 1943, when Ford's 3.5 million square-foot Willow Run was nearing its one-Liberator-an-hour peak output. It was a J model except for being built by Ford, so it received the "H" appellation.

After combat modifications in Alabama, it flew west to desolate Wendover, Utah, where its first crew, headed by Lt. George Reed, climbed aboard. Reed wound up commanding more missions in the aircraft—thirty—than any other pilot in its 137 mission career. Yes, that's 137 missions and not a single abort due to aircraft or crew issues (seven aborts were ordered by Group command).

Even more astonishing, on its missions, most of which were over Germany during the last explosive year of the war, not a single man aboard the aircraft was ever injured or killed.

No wonder they called her *Witchcraft*.

At the 1.8 million square-mile air base at Wendover, where a dozen Liberator bomb groups were trained, Reed and his crew (and "534" as the ship was known at the time) went through "phase" training: low-level flight, cross-country navigation, practice bomb runs, and gunnery strafing.

It was at Wendover that crew chief M/Sgt Joe Ramirez first laid eyes on 534. A stickler for maintenance, he polished instrument gauges and berated a co-pilot for an engine failure—even though they both knew he had nothing to do with it. Ramirez became so famous for his coddling of the aircraft that his group commander recommended him for the Bronze Star.

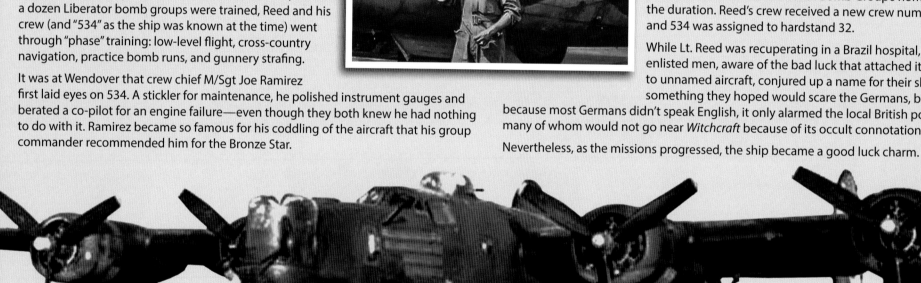

After a month of training in Wendover's whistling winter winds, Reed and Co. flew to Kansas, where Ramirez and his men boarded a train for New Jersey and transport by ship to Europe while the air crew flew on to Florida.

When they started south from Palm Beach two weeks later, it was two hours into the flight before Reed was allowed to open his sealed orders revealing their destination: the Eighth Air Force in England, via the southern route: the Caribbean, Brazil, French West Africa (Senegal), Morocco, and finally to Rackheath Army Air Field, Norfolk, England.

It was an uneventful flight, though Reed was in the hospital in Brazil for a week with strep throat and a cylinder failed over the Atlantic, shutting down an engine. No big deal.

Rackheath was a newly-built airfield with concrete runways and taxiways (a blessing in the wet and muddy English winter) and would be the 467th Bomb Group's home for the duration. Reed's crew received a new crew number (62), and 534 was assigned to hardstand 32.

While Lt. Reed was recuperating in a Brazil hospital, the enlisted men, aware of the bad luck that attached itself to unnamed aircraft, conjured up a name for their ship, something they hoped would scare the Germans, but because most Germans didn't speak English, it only alarmed the local British populace, many of whom would not go near *Witchcraft* because of its occult connotation.

Nevertheless, as the missions progressed, the ship became a good luck charm.

TAGGING ALONG

WITHIN THREE WEEKS of their arrival, Crew 62 joined 29 other ships of the 467th on its first mission: dropping 1,000-pounders on a Luftwaffe airfield at Bourges in central France. There was no flak, no ships were lost, and no attacking fighters were seen. The P-47 and P-51 escorts had nothing to do so they left to find targets of opportunity. A real milk run. Everyone thought the war wasn't going to be too bad after all.

But on the Group's tenth mission, things changed. The mission began late with a 1630 departure, timed so the bombers would be over the railroad marshalling yards at Hamm, Germany, just before sunset. Generally, the RAF bombed at night and the USAAF during the day, so there were usually a few hours of respite between the two visits that the Germans made good use of, sending out crews to repair the damage the previous bombers had inflicted. Mission #10 would put the Germans on notice to expect us at any time.

Witchcraft and 25 other bombers from the 465th hit Hamm without incident and with good results. Flak was heavy but no enemy aircraft were seen.

The sun was setting as the bombers crossed the Belgian coast on their way home. They'd been briefed that when it got dark they were to break formation, turn on their running lights, and get back to their home base on their own.

Unbeknownst to them, forty German Me-410 twin-engine heavy fighters used the declining dusk visibility to sneak in among the bombers and follow them back across the English Channel.

At 1000, as bombers began landing at various bases across East Anglia and the 467th's Liberators entered the landing pattern at Rackheath, the 410s attacked, downing two ships and killing seventeen men. Rounding quickly, they strafed the airfield and dropped 50-kg high explosive bombs, killing another man. Late-arriving bombers were dismayed to find every airfield in eastern England blacked out and their own anti-aircraft batteries lighting up the sky, thinking they were the enemy.

It must have been a fighter pilot's dream: to fly undetected at night among hundreds of unsuspecting enemy bombers, their running lights on and their guns secured.

Following this debacle, no more evening missions were flown over Germany.

CREW 62
Rear L to R: Henry Kubacek (g), Alex McClean (btg), Melvin Bland (ro), Vernon Bundrock (g), Robert McEwen (tg), Robert DeKerf (e, ttg).
Front L to R: John Oder (cp), George Reed (p), John Kramer (b).
Not pictured: Charles Mintzlaff (n).

DAY OF DAYS

FOR TWO DAYS leading up to D-Day, Crew 62 had bombed gun batteries on the French coast, completing their nineteenth and twentieth missions. Though they'd taken some flak hits, they'd been lucky and *Witchcraft* was getting a reputation as a ship that liked to fly and that crews liked to fly in.

6 June 1944 would be a busy day. Departure was at 0250 and Crew 62 arrived over coastal France well before dawn, dropping their 100-pound GP bombs from 15,000 feet through an unbroken cloud cover, led by a Pathfinder Force (PFF) radar-equipped ship. Because other bomber groups had been pounding French airfields for the last two weeks, no fighters were encountered, nor was any flak seen.

Five hours later they flew home watching the day dawn and the Channel congested with thousands of eastward-steaming ships. The airmen's hearts were filled with joy, watching their comrades taking the war to the Hun.

Back at Rackheath, they sprawled out on the warm grass and looked heavenward as dozens of bomber vees headed incessantly eastward.

And at 1630, they joined them for their second mission of the day, this time to bomb a railroad bridge at Pontaubault in Normandy, to prevent German troops from reaching the beaches Allied troops were storming.

Carrying 500-pound GP bombs, they hit the target from 15,000 feet with fair results. Though they saw no enemy aircraft, Allied planes were everywhere, and they all kept their eyes peeled. No one wanted to die on D-Day in a mid-air collision with a friendly.

An airman in the 791st Squadron expressed everyone's sentiments that day: "As we lay on our cots tonight and reflect on the day's happenings, we cannot help but think of the men who hit the beaches today. Here we are safe in our little huts and they are fighting and clawing to hold on to those sandy beaches! Our hearts go out to them, because we are fully aware that thousands of them will not be with us tomorrow."

SLOW AND STEADY...

AS ALLIED TROOPS advanced across France, so did their bomber support. Leading up to D-Day, the 467th hit airfields, aircraft factories, railways and marshalling yards, oil depots, and coastal gun emplacements, regularly putting up thirty planes on a mission. Losses were rare, averaging about one for every five missions, but still too many.

The Mighty Eighth, pounding enemy targets by day and the RAF doing the same at night, had reduced Luftwaffe strength. Even though the bomber crews routinely saw enemy fighters, they were rarely attacked, primarily because of their "little friends," the Thunderbolts and Mustangs, kept the enemy at bay.

Some missions were aborted due to bad weather. The famous English fog made takeoffs and forming up dangerous. Bomb groups flew out of a dozen airfields in East Anglia, their formation areas arrayed around the area perimeter like numbers on a clock, but with 500 bombers taking to the skies a dawn every day, it's a wonder more men didn't lose their lives before ever reaching their targets.

Weather affected bombing accuracy. The 467th encountered cloud obscuration on almost every mission, and it wasn't even winter yet. When Pathfinder aircraft dropped target flares, results were excellent; when no radar-equipped ships led the runs, results were often dismal.

Flak was usually light and inaccurate, but as more missions were flown over Germany, it got heavier and deadly accurate. On several missions, *Witchcraft* took flak hits.

Lt. Reed and Crew 62 completed their required thirty missions two weeks after D-Day, and Lt. Leonard Vogt and Crew 63 took *Witchcraft's* reins.

After the 467th Bomb Group had flown fifty missions, CO Col. Albert Shower examined gunnery records and made a startling discovery: the ball turrets' ammo use was well below the other guns, meaning the ball gunner rarely sighted the enemy. Shower decided to remove the one-ton turret. Doing so reduced the crew from ten to nine men, potentially saving a life; the weight reduction improved aircraft speed and fuel consumption; and the center of gravity moved forward. (The tail-heavy Liberator tended to fly in a nose-up attitude, decreasing the pilots' visibility and increasing their fatigue. Without a turret, it would be easier for them to keep the aircraft "on the step," flying straight and level.)

And though he violated Army Air Force regulations in doing so, Col. Shower's gutsy move was soon followed by other 2nd Air Division Liberator groups.

As summer ended, almost all of the 467th's bombing missions were over Germany, hitting railways, marshalling yards, airfields, and factories. For three weeks in October and November, the Group flew few combat missions. Instead, using 700-gallon rubber tanks installed in their bomb bays, most crews kept General Patton's 3rd Army supplied with gasoline as he raced across France. Despite the obvious danger of these flights, crews received no mission credit, as they were not flying over enemy territory.

A rare photo of *Witchcraft* showing all her identification markings. The circled "P" on the upper wing was the original 467th BG symbol.* In mid-1944 it was replaced by a red tail fin with a white diagonal stripe. The 790th Squadron "Q2" identifier is partially visible on the fuselage aft of the waist window. The individual aircraft identifier "M" is inside a white diagonal stripe on the fins and a portion of the serial number is on the inboard side of each vertical stabilizer.

The Rackheath Liberators await their next mission. Note the supply truck backed up to the second aircraft, likely unloading oxygen tanks or ammunition. In addition, some aircraft are painted while others show off shiny aluminum skins—a 300-pound savings in paint.

* The Germans often singled out groups, squadrons, and aircraft. To hinder identification, 8th AAF bomb groups were assigned letters and squadrons and an unrelated letter followed by a number.

WITCHCRAFT'S 100TH MISSION took place Christmas Eve day, 1944, in the largest armada of aircraft—2,000 bombers and 900 fighters—ever to take flight during the war, hitting targets during the Battle of the Bulge, Germany's last desperate offensive, taking place in the hilly and forested Ardennes Forest in Belgium and France.

Poor weather over the last few days had finally broken, and the 467th put up 62 Liberators, including their battered assembly ship. Only two Liberators remained at Rackheath due to mechanical issues. Each bomber carried 24 250-pound GP bombs. The Group assembled at Splasher Beacon 5 at 11,000 feet just before noon.

Their target was the railroad marshalling yard near Gerolstein, Germany, east of the Ardenne. They visually bombed from 22,000 feet and results were very good. Some flak was encountered but there were no enemy aircraft attacks. There were no losses during the bomb run, but *Battlin' Baby* had engine trouble and turned back early. As it neared its landing field in Norwich, waist gunner Denver Loberg fell out of the bomb bay while he was trying to salvo the bombs and was killed.

Given the unprecedented size of the attack, aircraft were still taking off in England when the first bombers began to hit their targets in Germany. It must have been a hellish experience for Germans that Christmas Eve as a seemingly endless stream of Liberators and Fortresses wreaked destruction on those who instigated the war.

On 29 March 1945, the 467th Bomb Group flew its 200th mission and Witchcraft its 129th. It had the additional notoriety of having fought in four major battles of the European Theater: the Battle of Normandy, Air Offensive Europe, the Battle of Northern France, and the Battle of Germany. At the celebration, Group commander Col. Albert Shower grew somber, saying, "While giving thanks for past success, let us be mindful of those who have not returned from these missions."

Witchcraft's final mission on 21 April to bomb a railroad junction in Salzburg, Austria, was aborted 130 miles from the target due to bad weather. The crew gingerly landed back at Rackheath with a full bomb bay—a rarity for this rare, unflappable bird.

On 10 June, *Witchcraft* flew west with Lt. Fred Jansen at the controls, along with his air and ground crew, including crew chief M/Sgt Joe Ramirez, its wheels finally rolling to a stop in front of the Willow Run Ford factory where, 18 months earlier, it had rolled off the line. For three months thereafter the ship was on display and thousands of people visited what had become one of the most famous aircraft of World War II.

Finally, on 16 September, *Witchcraft* made its final flight to Altus, OK, where it was unceremoniously scrapped. No pomp, no circumstance, and no good-byes. It was a tool that had served its purpose and was discarded.

But it should not have been and that's why the Collings Foundation's B-24J has been painted in *Witchcraft's* livery... so we will never forget what the men who flew this marvelous aircraft did: they saved the world.

Though smoke trails from the #2 engine, *Witchcraft* still finishes its 21 February 1945 bomb run, dropping four 500-pounders over Germany. (The smaller bombs were dropped by ship 201.)

After 130 credited missions, a battle-scarred *Witchcraft* sits on the Rackheath apron. Soon it will return to its birthplace at Willow Run, MI, where a celebration awaits.

STARTLING STATISTICS

- Combat missions: 137
- Credited combat missions: 130
- Aborts due to mission orders: 7
- Aborts due to aircraft or crew issues: 0
- Crews flying combat missions in the aircraft: 40
- Crewmen injured or killed in combat: 0
- Crewmen injured or killed in operational incidents: 0
- Combat flight time: 837 hours, 15 minutes
- Fuel used: 238,683 gallons
- Ordnance dropped: 608,000 pounds
- Engines replaced: 25
- Combat flak damage: 300 holes

WITCHCRAFT

PILOTS

There I was, a 19-year old kid in a brand-new airplane, heading for Hawaii. I remember starting out with an uneasy feeling. The Hawaiian Islands are 500 miles wide, but the Pacific is thousands of square miles and if your navigator didn't know his stuff, you could get into trouble real quick. But we came out right over Waikiki Beach. Our navigator brought us right on in.

You see, the Army had spent 18 months training me and they'd given me a good crew and a new airplane, but none of that mattered unless we had a good navigator. I couldn't have done it; no one else on our crew could have, really.

So you see, once you get the airplane flying, the most important person on the crew is not the pilot, but the navigator, who is the one who gets you to the target.

That's why I fired my first navigator, who almost flew us into a mountain. His job was just too important to risk everyone's life.

Omer "O.C." Kemp
Pilot
7th AAF / 494th BG / 865th BS

WHEN IT ENTERED THE WAR, the B-24 Liberator was the most complex machine in the world and one look at the instrument panel confirms this. Many a cadet sat in the left seat for the first time and wondered if he'd ever learn what all those switches and dials were for.

In addition, the Liberator was demanding and difficult to fly. One pilot said, "It was like flying a Mack truck," and another quipped, "Yeah, if that Mack truck had nine flat tires."

It was a true two-pilot aircraft. The co-pilot was as busy as the pilot, monitoring the engine gauges, running checklists, and doing everything else except flying the plane.

A Liberator crew usually consisted of four officers (pilot, co-pilot, navigator, and bombardier) and six enlisted men gunners, some of whom were also flight engineers and radio operators. Everyone, except the pilots, was dual rated so they could perform an incapacitated crewman's duties.

In addition, the pilot was "in command," responsible not only for the success of the mission, but also the safety of his crew. Army publications reminded him that he was in charge; he needed to work harder than anyone else; needed to know everyone's job; and was expected to dispense discipline. For many pilots, this was the hardest part of being in command: to maintain cordiality but not familiarity with the enlisted men, who might be less inclined to obey an order from a friend. But it was absolutely necessary.

Of course there were perks: officers had nifty uniforms and insignia. They were issued liquor, not beer. They received salutes and deference, being called "sir" or "captain." They messed and billeted separately from the enlisted men. And they got to fly the greatest aircraft in the world.

But the downside was the responsibility. It got around quickly if a pilot was confident or if he was tentative and fearful, though there were many things to fear. One of the biggest was the bomb run itself.

The pilot and co-pilot followed the navigator's headings toward the I.P. (Initial Point), where they then lined up on the target (usually less than 15 minutes away) at the correct speed, altitude, and heading. Then the fun began.

As they closed in on the target, the pilot and the bombardier adjusted the C-1 autopilot, at which point the bombardier, in the nose hunched over his bomb sight, peering through the lens, turned the bombsight left and right to keep the crosshairs lined up and the aircraft on track.

He was, in fact, flying the plane. Meanwhile, up on the flight deck, the pilots sat helpless, unable to touch the controls no matter what they saw coming at them, be it a sky black with flak or incoming fighters.

It was the longest two minutes of a man's life and one pilot said, "I would have gladly have traded being an officer if it meant I didn't have to go through that on every mission."

Douglas Page

EYE WITNESS

We were attached to the Air Transport Command, flying Liberators over the Hump (the Himalaya Mountains) during the monsoon, in the worst flying weather you can imagine, hauling gasoline from India to China.

We flew at 28,000 feet and often faced 100 mph winds. We had almost no navigation aids or maps, just a compass and a sextant, which the weather often rendered useless.

We once had an engine quit and though we had three others still running, we had to raise the nose and just "mush" along to maintain altitude, flying between the mountain peaks.

On any given day, we would lose 15-20 planes because the weather was so bad and the mountains were so high.

Most of us were patriotic. I was willing to die for my country. I looked in the mirror and said, "You're a dead duck, so enjoy your life, go do your job, your country calls."

I was lucky and made it home.

John Polder
Navigator
10th AAF, 7th BG, 9th BS

NAVIGATOR

THOUGH HE WAS RELEGATED to a tiny desk facing the pilots' feet down in the crowded nose compartment, as we've seen, the navigator was—especially over the seemingly endless Pacific Ocean—the most important person on the crew and had an array of instruments as befitted his status.

Navigators used four methods (or a combination thereof) to determine the aircraft's geographic position. Each method had its strengths and weaknesses.

- Celestial: sighting the sun or stars with a sextant.
- Radio: broadcast signals received by a radio compass.
- Pilotage: comparing a map with terrain and landmarks.
- Dead reckoning: using a compass, ground speed, a clock, and an initial known position to fix location.

A sextant allowed the navigator to "shoot his fixes" and figure azimuth, and with that and accurate time, the aircraft's course. Cloud obscuration vitiated this method, as did aircraft instability caused by turbulence.

The radio compass received medium frequency signals from a beacon broadcasting a station identifier, which could be honed in on by comparing signal strength over time as the aircraft moved closer or father away. Of course, the enemy didn't broadcast these "Here I am!" signals.

Pilotage and dead reckoning were difficult enough over land, but over water pilotage was useless and dead

reckoning involved using white caps by day and flame floats by night, whose directional movement were noted.

The drift meter, a floor-mounted, downward-looking telescope, aided dead reckoning. The pilot flew 60° to starboard for three minutes, then flew 60° to port for another three minutes, finally turning back to his original track. During these three courses, the navigator rotated the parallel lines in the drift meter eyepiece until the objects on the ground (or the whitecaps on the ocean) moved parallel to the lines. This "three-course wind" method yielded drift angle due to winds aloft, which was used to calculate course and ground speed and thus position.

A sophisticated magnetic compass called a "gyro-stabilized flux gate" compass had a sensitive magnetic field detector mounted on the aircraft's wing tip which provided accurate magnetic north indications. Connected with the autopilot, it allowed the ship to fly a steady course.

Prior to flight, it was the navigator's duty to calibrate the altimeter, compasses, airspeed indicators, and the drift meter. He also checked his sextant and watch for accuracy.

His job was the most taxing of the entire crew and his competence meant the difference between life and death, whether over enemy territory or the emptiness of the great oceans.

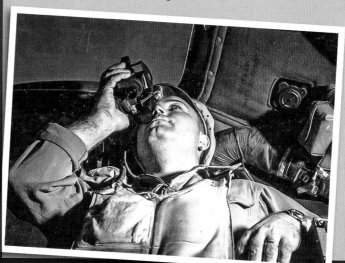

ABOVE The Fairchild Model A-10-A sextant featured battery power, a drum micrometer, gyroscope, bubble gauge, and an artificial horizon.

Douglas Page

ABOVE The navigator's desk is hinged to tilt up. He's facing backwards, seated on a swivel stool, facing his navigational instruments. Note the oxygen and heating connections, center left.

BOMBARDIER

The Norden bombsight functioned like a carpenter's level. If the bubbles were off center by a fraction, at high altitudes the bombs could go way off target. Bumps or shifts in wind could move the bubbles.

The pilot and navigator would get us within fifteen minutes of the objective and then I'd try to get visual contact. As we approached, I'd go back and pull the safety pins from the bombs. Then I'd go forward and zero in with the bombsight, making quick compensations to get those bubbles back on dead center and stay there.

Some of the bombardiers "toggled," dropping their bombs when the plane in front of them dropped his. I never did—I did my own calculations and cross-hair sighting and though it may have looked like I dropped my bombs when the lead plane did, my drop was always based on my calculations.

One time, the lead bombardier dropped all his bombs in the water, completely missing the target. I learned to never, ever depend on the lead.

Jack Berger
Bombardier
7th AAF / 494th BG / 865th BS

DUTCH EMIGRE CARL NORDEN started working on ship gyrostabilizers in 1904 and during WWI, his aircraft gyroscope greatly advanced leveling and wind bombing issues. As larger bombers came into play, the pilot and the bombardier had interconnected pilot direction indicator (PDI) dials, so as the bombardier sighted, the pilot would match his course. Norden used the entire bombsight as the indicator, using a linkage from the bombsight (called the "football" because of its shape) to an autopilot that controlled flight axes. If the cables to the aircraft control surfaces were damaged, the autopilot could fly the aircraft using electric impulses to servos on the ailerons, rudders, and elevators.

The football contained a telescope attached to a gyroscope that kept the sight pointed at the same azimuth regardless of aircraft movement. Azimuth is an angular measurement in a spherical coordinate system. The vector from an observer to a point of interest (like a star) is projected downward onto the horizon; the angle between that point on the horizon and due north is the azimuth, measured in degrees.

To time bomb drops, Norden refined the "equal distance" concept, based on the observation that the time needed to travel a certain distance over the ground remains relatively constant during the bomb run. After locating the target in the sight, the bombardier makes fine adjustments with two control wheels. An internal calculator settles on a solution in just a few seconds, reducing the required length of the bomb run to just thirty seconds.

But there were practical problems. When bombers flew tight formations, each using his own bombsight, the autopilots vectored the planes toward each other as they approached the target, threatening collision. This was resolved by having just the lead bombardier sight the bomb run, the rest salvoing their bombs when they saw the lead drop his.

But if he was wrong, everyone was wrong.

Real-world results were mixed. The bombsight required visual contact. In addition, jet stream winds at high altitude overwhelmed the mechanism. Even the shape and the paint on a bomb affected its trajectory. Nevertheless, the Norden bombsight was a piece of remarkable technology that helped win the war.

It was also the beneficiary of an ad campaign that greatly overstated its capabilities. Photos of armed guards escorting the sight to and from bombers in England added to its mystique. Those who used the competing Sperry bombsight believed it was just as capable as the more renowned Norden.

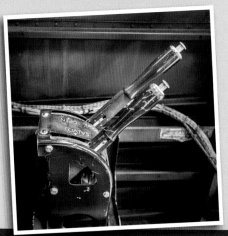

CENTER Bomb bay door and emergency bomb salvo levers.

ABOVE In the event of a landing in enemy territory, bombardiers swore to defend its secret with their lives.

Douglas Page

One time our bomb doors opened only partway and got stuck—so, as we had been instructed, we dropped our bombs right through them. Of course that caused the bomb doors to flop around and the B-24 started buffeting. That forced us out of formation, which we hated—there was safety in numbers and German fighters pounced on stragglers.

As flight engineer I used a four-foot-long stick to measure gasoline before we took off, and each of our bomb arming wires had a loop on the end of it. I rigged up one of those wires to the end of my gas stick and cautiously walked out onto the catwalk. I had an oxygen bottle but no parachute—there wasn't enough room. Other than the narrow metal beam, there was nothing but open sky beneath my feet. Fortunately, I was able to loop those bomb doors, pull them up, and secure them. So we were able to get back in formation.

That was one of the hairiest missions.

George Clay Henry
Flight Engineer
15th AAF, 449th BG, 716th BS

FLIGHT ENGINEER

THE LIBERATOR is such a complex aircraft that two pilots aren't enough; a third person is required to get and keep the aircraft airborne: the Flight Engineer.

Though he was an enlisted man, he had crucial flight deck responsibilities. He was often the Crew Chief, a liaison between the officers and the enlisted men. As such, he was in charge of seeing to it that the aircraft was maintained, fueled, oiled, and ready to fly when the time came.

At start-up, the FE stood in front of the #3 engine (nearest to the co-pilot), which was always started first, as it powered the ship's hydraulics. He checked for fire, fuel and oil leaks, pedestrians, and anything else that might inhibit normal and safe operation.

Once the engines were purring, he pulled the wheel chocks, removed the "pogo" or kickstand under the empennage, and disappeared into the bomb bay.

When next seen he was perched in a hatch just behind the pilots, intently scanning the surroundings to ensure that the Liberator's 100-foot long wings didn't hit anything during taxi. This is because from where the pilots sat, level with the engines, they could not see the wing tips.

During the take-off run-up, the FE checked generator loads. When the pilots tested the feathering capabilities of each propeller (which changed the angle of attack of a prop on a problematic or damaged engine so it didn't inhibit flight), the FE checked his meters for the proper load.

During flight, the FE kept track of engine performance: oil pressure and temperature, cylinder head and carburetor temperature, and fuel consumption. He also ensured better engine fuel consumption by synchronizing the propellers, setting the correct RPM and then visually sighting the far engine's yellow prop tip through the near engine's turning radius. When the props were synchronized, the far prop stopped moving inside the disk of the near prop. A really good FE could do this by simply listening to the engines.

He was also in charge of keeping the bomb bay doors open over target as they had a tendency to creep closed, preventing the bombs from releasing.

Among his many duties, he was qualified for co-pilot duties, the parachute officer, the first aid specialist, and the assistant radio operator.

 ABOVE RIGHT Each engine could be assigned a different fuel tank. Ammeters, a voltmeter selector switch, and four generator switches were monitored by the FE, along with instrument panel gauges.

Jonathan Sabin

As we were heading back to England, we got a call from a base requesting that we broadcast the proper IFF (Identification Friend or Foe). There were two Spitfires right with us, ready to knock us down if I didn't give them the signal because the Germans would patch up crashed planes and sneak into our formations as they were returning home. I gave them the proper IFF signal and the Spits escorted us right in.

We were pretty banged up and the pilot was having trouble getting enough airspeed for landing so he said anybody who wanted to bail out, could. I had bailed out once before and didn't want to do it again, so I asked him what he was going to do and he said, "I'm going to bring this thing in" and I said, "Okay, I'm going to stay with you."

We had no hydraulics so I had to go down and throw the nose wheel down, hoping it would lock on its own. Then I fired off a couple of red flares so they'd know to get ready for us.

We got down okay.

That was our first mission.

Clem Leone
Radio Operator
8th AAF, 445th BG, 700th BS

RADIO OPERATOR

DURING THE WAR, radios were large, heavy, and hot and only bombers could carry a full complement of radio equipment.

The B-24 radio operator sat at a small wooden table behind the co-pilot, facing starboard. On the table was a liaison receiver. "Liaison" equipment allowed communication with the ground while "command" equipment—an entirely separate system—was used to communicate with nearby aircraft. There was also an "interphone" system allowing communication between the aircraft crew.

A large liaison transmitter unit sat under the table. Two antenna tuning units were situated aft of the pilot and an antenna tuning unit and frequency meter, both the size of oversized shoeboxes, were affixed aft of the operator's table.

Command radio equipment was located in a compartment above the wing over the rear bomb bay. In later Liberators, the radioman was moved there so the navigator could take his position on the flight deck, nearer the pilots.

On the desk was a Morse key, which could be secured in the "send" position if a crash was imminent, allowing rescuers to "fix" the aircraft location using the constant signal even after the crew had bailed out.

The aircraft employed several antennas for reception and transmission, including the high-frequency Radio Directional Finder (RDF), commonly called a "loop" antenna, which could be rotated to maximize signal gain. The loop was enclosed in a teardrop-shaped fairing, as seen atop *Witchcraft's* fuselage aft of the wing.

A drawback to early RDF was that the antenna gain was the same whether the signal was coming from the front or the back of the antenna, so unless you had a general idea of your geographic location in relation to the broadcast signal, you might follow the signal in the exact opposite direction, as the *Lady Be Good* navigator did. (*See* page 45.)

Long Range Navigation (LORAN), Very High Frequency (VHF) and Ultra High Frequency (UHF) signal technology advanced during the war, greatly improving navigational capabilities. Of course your cell phone has far better geographic locating capabilities than any technology available at that time.

There was also a 300-foot trailing antenna for the liaison transmitter, at the end of which was affixed the "avocado," a lead weight intended to reduce whipping in the airstream. An electric reel spooled the antenna when not in use. On occasion, radio operators forgot to reel in the avocado on landing, causing substantial damage to the aircraft.

In addition to his regular duties, the radio operator was trained as a waist gunner, an assistant flight engineer, a first aid specialist, and a top turret gunner.

EYE WITNESS

We were hit by flak over Vienna, losing our two inboard engines. We pitched down, the blue dome of St. Karlskirche rising fast to meet us. I looked over my shoulder and through the window saw the bombardier and navigator crawling aft. I tried calling the pilot on the intercom but it had been knocked out. I was locked inside my turret with no way out and no parachute.

We were losing altitude and the Austrian Alps loomed before us. Separated from the formation, we were now sitting ducks.

I scanned the horizon for enemy fighters. Two black dots at two o'clock high were headed straight for us. Seconds passed but they did not attack. Then I recognized the red tails—the Tuskegee P-51s!

They approached us warily—some trigger-happy gunners had fired at them in the past—and fell into formation with us, waggling their wings. They escorted us home safely.

Achilles Kozakis
Nose Gunner
15th AAF, 451st BG, 726th BS

NOSE TURRET GUNNER

THE FIRST LIBERATORS had a "greenhouse" nose, a glazing with no forward guns. It didn't take long before the Germans discovered this key defensive weakness, and head-on attacks brought many planes down early in the war.

In response, a single .50-caliber machine gun was mounted above the bomb-aiming window in B-24Ds. The gunner, straddling the bombardier, interfered with bomb sighting, so the gun was moved to a location below the window. From this position, it was manned by the bombardier, but sometimes it was fixed and wired to be fired by the pilot. Two cheek guns were added in later D models. Unfortunately, even with three guns in the nose, the Liberator's up-front firepower was still inadequate because the nose compartment was too cramped to use them effectively and their fields of fire were limited.

Meanwhile, in Australia, enterprising 5th AAF engineers grafted a Consolidated A-6 tail turret onto a B-24D nose, which proved so successful in battle that field depots all over the world were soon scavenging tail turrets from wrecked aircraft and installing them as nose turrets.

Now fully committed to a nose turret on the Liberator, the Army gave the Emerson company just 100 days to convert their tail turret to a nose turret. Installation of the resulting electric A-15 turret (which included bullet-resistant glass) required scores of changes to the B-24D airframe, including an all-new bombardier station and outward-opening nose gear doors. It also added 200 pounds to the nose, a welcome center-of-gravity change in a tail-heavy aircraft. It was also electric (24 volts) while the Consolidated A-6 turret used the ship's main hydraulic system for power.

But once it went into production, Emerson had trouble keeping up with orders, so Convair* installed its A-6 series tail turret in its Liberator noses until Emerson caught up.

By the spring of 1944, Liberators were rolling off all five production lines with the Emerson nose turret, giving the bomber more than enough forward firepower to make any fighter pilot think twice about a head-on attack.

Since fighters stopped attacking as bomber formations entered the "flak zone" near the target and didn't continue the attack until the bomb run was completed, the bombardier often did double duty as a nose gunner as well.

When assigned to the turret, the gunner was also designated a "turret specialist" and made the assistant to the Armament Officer, usually the bombardier.

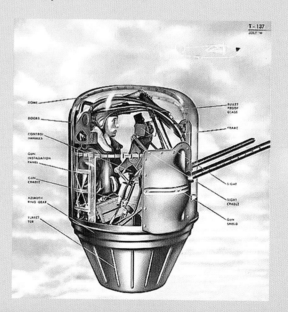

ABOVE LEFT 2nd Lt Joseph Orley examines bullet holes in the nose turret of *Wells Cargo*, a B-24H in the 723rd BS, 450th BG, 15th AAF.

* In late 1941, Reuben Fleet sold his interest in Consolidated to Vultee Aircraft. On 17 March 1943 the two merged to form Consolidated-Vultee Aircraft, known as "Convair."

EYE WITNESS

I was the flight engineer and also the top turret gunner. My turret was located right between four large engines. I had two .50-caliber machine guns firing inches from my head. It was noisy... but so was the airplane!

We had cut-offs to keep us from firing into parts of our own airplane, but I remember this one wire antennae, strung from just behind my turret to the top of one of the vertical stabilizers; I would keep shooting that thing off.

Our ball turret gunner was a crack shot and destroyed at least five German fighters. But the confirmation process for crediting kills was so very complicated that after the first couple of times, he didn't even bother putting in claims.

During one mission our bombardier accidentally knocked my intercom loose. So I didn't get any fighter warnings. I was looking toward the tail when the Germans attacked from the front, out of the sun. They went right through and shot down the B-24s on either side of us. Boy, I really screwed up there.

George Clay Henry
Top Turret Gunner
15th AAF, 449th BG, 716th BS

TOP TURRET GUNNER

THE FIRST LIBERATOR model, the B-24A, which was declared by the British to be unsuitable for combat due to its lack of self-sealing fuel tanks, nevertheless had a pair of .30-caliber machine guns in the tail and four .50-caliber machine guns in the nose, belly, and both waist positions.

But it didn't have a dorsal or a ball turret, the lack of which became immediately apparent as soon as the first models were delivered to the British as Liberator Mark Is.

The British corrected the problem by installing a Boulton-Paul turret with four .303 machine guns aft of the wing in their Liberator IIs while the Americans, in their nearly identical LB-30s, installed a Martin A-3 electric turret located above the flight deck just behind the pilots.

The turret was usually manned by the flight engineer, though the radio operator would also pitch in if needed. If the crew had at least ten men, an enlisted gunner was often assigned to the turret.

For obvious reasons, the gunners were all trained to work any of the gun positions on a Liberator. Those assigned primarily to nose, top, ball, or tail turrets were termed "turret gunners" while those manning the guns in the waist were called "flexible gunners." In addition, the bombardier and navigator were also gunnery-trained and one of them often did double duty as the gunnery officer, ensuring that the enlisted men knew their duties and kept their stations and guns in clean, working order.

The electric A-3 top turret was equipped with twin .50-caliber Browning M-2 machine guns. The hinged seat dropped down and the operator pulled himself up into the turret, the seat being locked under him. The turret rotated 360° and the arc of elevation of the guns was more than 90°. When facing to the rear, the Liberator's split tail was in the top turret line of fire so an interrupter circuit was installed to prevent the gunner accidentally shooting the tail surfaces.

The A-3 was a tight squeeze, however, and gunners soon complained. A taller "high hat" turret, designated the A-3D was designed by Martin and first installed in the B-24H.

One of the enlisted men (usually a waist gunner) was designated Senior Armorer. He assisted the bombardier in arming the bombs or dispensing thin aluminum strips called "chaff" or "window," which confused enemy radar.

On 28 September 1944, we bombed the Krupp works at Magdeburg, Germany. Waves of twenty enemy fighters attacked our box of twelve ships from the seven o'clock position. There seemed to be hundreds of them. I got my sight on the nearest one and blasted away. I saw fire and smoke come out of his engine and saw the dead pilot, his oxygen mask torn off. The whole ship was vibrating from everyone shooting. Most of our planes were blazing and burning.

We were hit over fifty times, holes everywhere. Every direction I looked, flak was bursting. I must have prayed out loud. I could smell flak through my oxygen mask and was sweating even at 40° below zero.

The ship on our left got a direct hit in the nose and almost crashed into us, a man's body hanging half way out of what was left of the nose. In the ball I was practically looking the bursts in the face as they tracked us along. Flak kept exploding right under me.

John Briol
Ball Turret Gunner
8th AAF / 457th BG / 748th BS

BALL TURRET GUNNER

THE B-24A HAD no ventral guns; the first variant to have armament protecting the ship's belly was the B-24C, in which a single .50-caliber machine gun, known as a "tunnel"gun, was mounted where the aft floor hatch is in *Witchcraft*. But the gunner could hardly see a thing and the small scanning windows added in D models on each side of the fuselage did little to help.

The next idea, first seen in the B-24D, was a Bendix retractable and remotely-sighted two-gun belly turret over which a gunner hunched, looking through a periscope. The turret worked but gave the gunners motion sickness and the tunnel gun was restored after less than 300 installations.

It was finally determined that the only solution was a manned turret like the twin .50-caliber A-2 Sperry ball turret (manufactured by Briggs) first used in the B-17E.

Its key drawback was that it was fixed to a ring in the aircraft floor, which allowed a 360° turning radius, but its hatch was accessible only when the guns were pointed straight down. If the turret incurred battle damage that prevented upward rotation, the occupant was trapped inside for the duration of the flight. And if either of the main gear sustained damage and could not fully extend, the gunner was exposed to a horrific dragging death during landing.

The specially-adapted Briggs/Sperry A-13 ball turret first appeared on the B-24D and became standard on the G model. Another advantage of the deep-bellied Liberator fuselage was that it allowed room for a hydraulic lift which fully retracted the electric turret, protecting the gunner no matter the condition of the aircraft landing gear. If the hydraulics failed, an electric winch or a hand pump raised the turret, and the gunner, to safety.

The turret itself appears smaller than it is. A ball turret gunner related that when he joined the Army Air Force, he did not have to duck to go under a string that had been tied between two door jambs. He was directed to one side and found himself in a room with a others his same height. It suddenly occurred to him that he had just volunteered to be a ball gunner.

There wasn't room in the sphere for a seat parachute, so gunners often left it in the waist or wore a chest parachute. And though there was an outlet to plug in a heated suit, the gunner couldn't fit inside while wearing one.

The M-2 machine guns were belt-fed from ammo boxes resting on the top of the turret. The guns themselves were mounted on either side of the turret level with the gunner's head, which left many operators nearly deaf after the war.

We stood at open windows and swung our machine guns at any enemy aircraft that came into range. The ship was loud to begin with but when the fighters came in all hell broke loose and the guns throughout the ship boomed away. If a German fighter got hit, it was often hard to tell who had hit him.

It was cold at altitude, sometimes -40° F. The wind howled through the fuselage and the barrel of my .50-caliber whistled in the slipstream. Frost formed an exposed surfaces. We had heavy wool and leather suits and gloves, but the cold still got to you and many guys experienced frostbite. Our heated flight suits were plugged into an electrical outlet near our position. They were pretty rudimentary by today's standards and many shorted out, sometimes burning our skin.

Missions were hours long and we learned to put cans of food under our clothes so they would not freeze. That way we had something to eat on the way home.

Richard Weber
Waist Gunner
15th AAF / 460th BG / 763rd BS

WAIST GUNNERS

FOLLOWING WORLD WAR ONE, General John Pershing asked John Browning to scale up the .30-06 machine gun. The result was the M-2 (or "Ma Deuce" as the troops called it) air-cooled .50-caliber machine gun, the final version of which proved so effective that it is still in use today, almost a hundred years later.

The 60-pound gun operates on the short recoil principle, firing up to 850 rounds per minute, yielding long range, accuracy, and immense stopping power. The M-2 was used in all U.S. aircraft and ground forces during the war. The British stuck with the .303-caliber, which resulted in some difficulty adapting Liberator gun stations early in the war.

The first three Liberator variants had no waist guns, only small observation windows. But beginning with the B-24D, the windows were enlarged and the light-barrel AN/M-2 was mounted on a moveable pivot centered in each window.

But with the guns opposite each other, the B-24's narrow fuselage resulted in collisions as the gunners tracked attacking fighters. Starting with the B-24J, waist gun mounts were moved to the fore and aft lower corners of opposing windows. This still proved problematic and by the H model, the windows themselves were staggered to minimize gunners interfering with each other in the heat of battle.

Also on the H model, the windows were finally enclosed with Plexiglas. With temperatures over northern Europe at 25,000 feet plummeting to -60° F, a gunner at an open window could get frostbite in minutes. Silk gloves worn under heavy woolen mittens allowed them to handle their guns without losing skin, and the cold temps kept the barrels from melting down, but it was nevertheless incredibly dangerous duty.

The cartridges in the Liberator were belt-fed, the bullets pressed into metal linkages and layered in loops in wooden boxes* carrying up to 600 rounds. A gunner could burn through his entire supply in under a minute, which gave birth to the phrase: "the whole nine yards," used when a person has exhausted all his options. The "nine yards" refers to the length of the .50-caliber machine gun belt of the P-51 Mustang fighter, which just happens to be 27 feet long. So when you've gone through the "whole nine yards," you're in big trouble. Of course the cartridge belts in the Liberator are substantially longer, but the same principle applies.

Since the guns were manually-operated (without an electric feed boost), the top turret machine gun interference circuit was unavailable and thus it was possible for an excited or inexperienced gunner to shoot the split tail's horizontal stabilizer or vertical fin and rudder. To remedy this, metal cables inhibiting the firing arc were installed at the factory. Of course, the very first thing the gunners in the fight did was to remove the restricting cables. Nevertheless, there were very few cases of this sort of self-inflicted damage as a gunner who did so soon found himself relegated to a ground crew.

* The ammo box also served as a stand under the rear fuselage to prevent a parked Liberator from settling on its tail-heavy hind end.

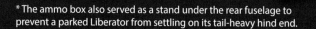

ABOVE CENTER .50-caliber bullet (actual size). Caliber is the measurement across the base of the projectile; in this case, one-half an inch.

Thomas O'Neil

EYE WITNESS

Our target on 17 April 1944 was the railroad marshalling yards at Sofia, Bulgaria, and it was really a thriller.

When we started our bomb run we encountered heavy flak. We were "Tail-end Charlie" of our formation and after bombs away, two Me-109s came down at us. I poured lead into the first one and all of a sudden he exploded right before my eyes. Sure was a funny feeling to see it.

One of the other B-24s was also firing at the 109 and he put several holes in our #1 engine. Oil started pouring out and it looked like we would have a fire, but quick thinking by "Ace," our pilot, stopped it and kept the engine working.

During interrogation after the mission we found out that the tail gunner who had shot up our ship was also claiming the fighter I got, even though it was impossible for anyone but me to have gotten him and there are three witnesses to that fact. We'll put in our claim and it goes to wing headquarters who will decide who gets it.

I know he was mine and that's what counts.

Marshall Kottler
Tail Gunner
15th AAF / 87th BG / 415th BS

TAIL TURRET GUNNER

EXTENSIVE PLANNING WENT into designing the Liberator's expansive bomb bay, but protecting the plane itself (and the men in it) seemed to be almost an afterthought. It wasn't until air crews demanded protection that cockpits began to be armored and turrets added and improved.

The tail of the Liberator was particularly vulnerable. The B-24A had twin .50-caliber machine guns mounted in a simple Plexiglas enclosure with sliding doors, between which the guns jutted.

The B-24C was the first version to be fitted with the hydraulically-powered Consolidated A-6* turret, which had two .50-caliber machine guns staggered fore and aft so their fire pattern would line up as the turret rotated. The tinted, slanted sighting window was one of the identifying characteristics of the A-6 series turret.

The A-6A added fairings around the machine guns to reduce drag. Like all turrets, the tail turret started out heavy and slow, but attacking fighters were anything but and as usual, theater needs were soon relayed back in the ZI (Zone of the Interior: America). A lighter version, known as the MPC A-6B

(designed by Consolidated but built by Motor Products), was developed and first installed on the B-24G models. It had symmetrical (not staggered) guns and larger Plexiglas side windows that increased visibility.

Beginning with the B-24L, an attempt was made to reduce the weight of the now too-heavy Liberator by 1,000 pounds. Thus, two hand-held, hydraulically-assisted M-6A "Stinger" guns were mounted in the tail, protected by a large Plexiglas housing offering the best visibility yet of any tail turret, but the least protection for the gunner.

In addition to his duties in the tail turret, the gunner was also a turret specialist and assistant to the parachute officer, who was usually the flight engineer.

Apart from frostbite, flak, and fighters, the tail gunner braved yet another danger: when crew members used the relief tube, the external Venturi tube would spray urine down the fuselage, some of which would find its way into the gaps between the empennage and the turret. Many a crew member was warned—in the strongest terms—to not use the relief tube when the tail turret was manned.

* "A" for automatic (powered) control, "M" for manual (non-powered). The "6" represents Consolidated's 6th design. Refinements receive a letter appellation.

ABOVE Both the graphic and the photo are of MPC A-6B turrets, identical to the one on *Witchcraft* (right).

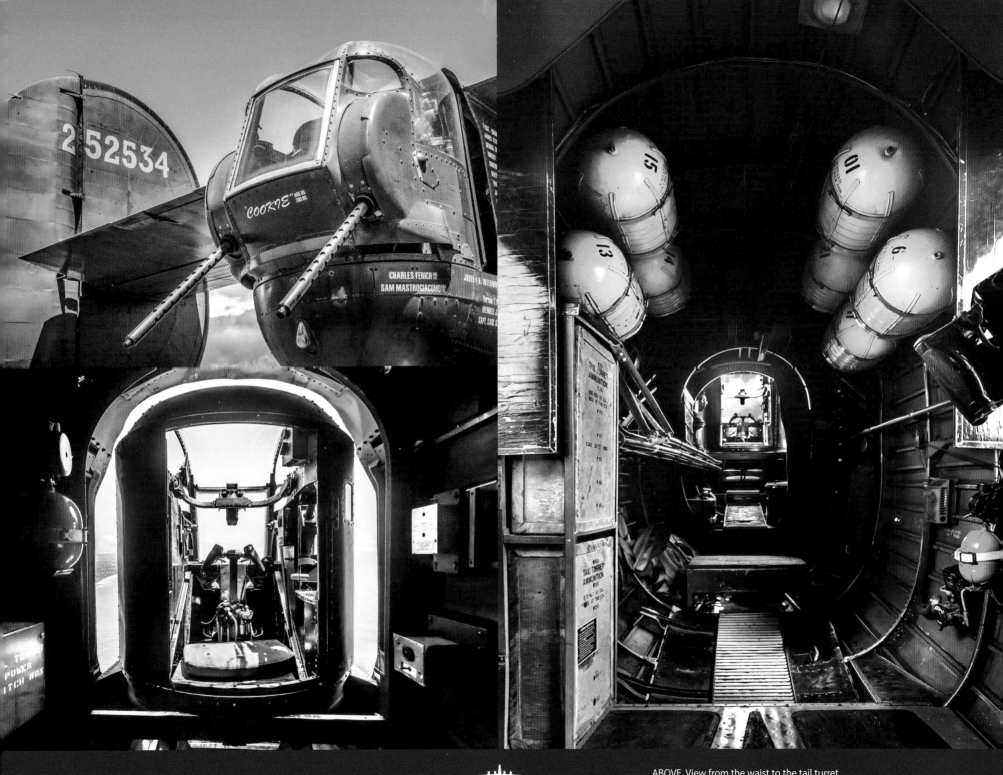

ABOVE View from the waist to the tail turret,
which has to be the loneliest position of the war.

SURVIVAL

THE LIBERATOR WAS, quite simply, a bomb delivery device, uninsulated, unpressurized, uncomfortable, and unsafe. Every exposed piece of metal wanted to cut you. Most crew members didn't even have seats, much less seat belts.

Above 10,000 feet, oxygen was required. Each of the 24 yellow lozenge-shaped canisters held 400 psi of pressurized oxygen, which was fed through a demand-flow system of regulators and masks to the crew. A "blinker" gauge indicated oxygen flow. When a crewman moved around the plane, he carried a green portable oxygen tank with him. But pressurized oxygen is dangerous and the metal tanks and equipment were bulky and heavy.

Personal hygiene solutions were basic. A bucket with a lid was the stool and a rubber relief hose with an external Venturi tube disposed of urine externally. A popular prank was to plug the tube, with predictable results.

Each crewman wore a parachute harness. The chest parachute pack was stowed near the crewman's station (or used as seat padding). When the bail out bell rang, it was clipped onto the harness. After bailing out, a large red "D" ring was pulled to pop the chute.

Over Europe in winter, temperatures at 25,000 feet were -60° F. Over their long-john underwear and flight suits, crewmen wore padded suits which plugged into 24v outlets. They concentrated heat in uncomfortable areas like behind the knees and, like old-fashioned Christmas trees, if the circuit was broken anywhere, the entire suit ceased to function.

Over the heated suit, the gunners wore flak* vests, steel plates encased in ballistic nylon weighing twenty pounds. In the drafty turrets and at the open waist windows, it was so cold flesh would stick to metal, so the men wore silk gloves under thick woolen mittens. Frostbite was common among gunners in the European Theater.

Imagine trying to negotiate the nine-inch wide catwalk through the bomb bay in this sort of battle dress. Nearly impossible, and if you had to bail out, you had to first shed the flak vest, then the gloves and heavy insulated boots, and finally the heated suit, then find where you stowed your parachute, attach it, and then make your way to either the rear hatch, the nose wheel doors, or the bomb bay.

The Liberator has two compartments above the wing containing two five-man life rafts, manually released via cable. The rafts carried rations, water, sea water distillers, green dye, reflecting mirrors, flares, and most importantly, a Gibson Girl radio, an emergency transmitter with a box-kite antenna. The radio was held between the knees and turning the crank sent out a Morse Code SOS signal.

Named after the curvaceous models popularized by a Madison Avenue artist named Gibson (whose employer sold girdles), the radio had a secondary, perhaps even more important, value: it was water tight and saved many a downed airman's life as he clung to his "girl" and waited for the Navy "Dumbos" (PBY Catalinas) to find and rescue him.

* An abbreviation of the German word "Fliegerabwehrkanone" (aircraft-defense gun). Flak projectiles contained shards of metal capable of cutting through skin, fuel tanks, and engines.

BOMB BAY

WHEN REUBEN FLEET said he could build a better bomber than the B-17, he meant twice as good, as in having two bomb bays instead of one. The shoulder-mounted Davis wing made a tall, wide bomb bay possible. 8,000 pounds of bombs, 500-pound GP (General Purpose), 100-pound incendiary, or 2,000-pound bunker-busters could fit inside a bomb bay that allowed better access to the ordnance than any other bomber.

The catwalk on the box-section keel separates the bomb racks and is only nine inches wide, but the average man in the early 1940s was just 5'8" tall and weighted just 145 pounds. (Today, navigating it is an incentive for us well-fed folks to go on a diet.)

The wing center section (which is an immense fuel tank) forms the ceiling of the forward bomb bay, which presents a tempting target for attackers who knew if they could start a fire there, it would quickly spread to the bomb bay and down the B-24. Hence the top gunner's position forward of the wing, to discourage just such attempts. The aft portion of the bay sits under the radio equipment compartment. Rubber fuel tanks could be placed in the fore section while the aft portion still carried bombs.

Unlike the outward-hinged bomb bay doors on the B-17 (which cut airspeed by ten knots), the Liberator had hydraulically-operated sliding doors of corrugated aluminum, which hug the hull when open, with minimal impact on air speed. (The inventor reportedly donated the proceeds of his roll-top patent to the war effort.)

The doors were designed to be kicked off their tracks if necessary, which meant they are lightweight and cannot bear a person's weight. They also resulted in the poor ditching characteristics of the Liberator. Upon impact they collapse, the keel gives way, the aircraft breaks in two aft of the wing, and the plane sinks rapidly. Many crews preferred to limp home with almost no chance of a safe landing rather than risk it.

ARMORERS

WHILE THE CREW SLEPT, the armorers retrieved the bombs chosen for the mission from revetments (bomb storage areas surrounded by tall earthen banks), placing them on trolleys and hauling them to the aircraft, where they then attached the guidance fins to the tail of each bomb. At this point, the bombs (containing RDX, an explosive nitroamine, or plastic explosive) were still relatively safe because they lacked fuzes.

Once the bombs were secured on their shackles on the bomb bay racks, an armorer then carefully screwed a cylindrical fuze into the bomb's nose. The fuze had a small propeller (the "arming vane") at the tip, which was prevented from spinning by a cotter pin. Inside the fuze was a spike which, upon impact, was either mechanically or electrically driven into a small detonation charge that triggered the main bomb explosive. Once the fuze was secured, any jolt or impact on the bomb could detonate it. Armorers moved slowly and deliberately, but horrific accidents did happen.

Once aloft, as the bomber passed the Initial Point, the bombardier entered the bomb bay and removed the cotter pins from each propeller, showing the pins to the pilots as he returned to this station in the nose. There he threw the lever that opened the bomb bay doors, sighted the target through its final moments, and flipped the bomb release switches, at which point the bombs were released and the tiny propellers on the nose started spinning some 200 revolutions, driving a screw that pushed the spike into the detonator charge. Well away from the bomber by now, the bomb was fully armed and would explode on impact.

Sometimes the bomb shackles failed to work properly and bombs got hung-up on the racks or in the bomb bay, at which point the bombardier or some other lucky soul had to kick or pry them out. If the cotter pins were still in place, good. If they were not, they either had to be replaced before attempting to clear the bomb or the greatest care imaginable had to be taken in so doing.

All that being said, about one in six bombs dropped failed to detonate because of faulty fuzes, arming propellers, or explosives.

ABOVE This armorer wears his ballcap with the bill up for three reasons: (1) to keep him from parting his skull on low-clearance interiors, (2) the officers hated it, and (3) it just looked cool.

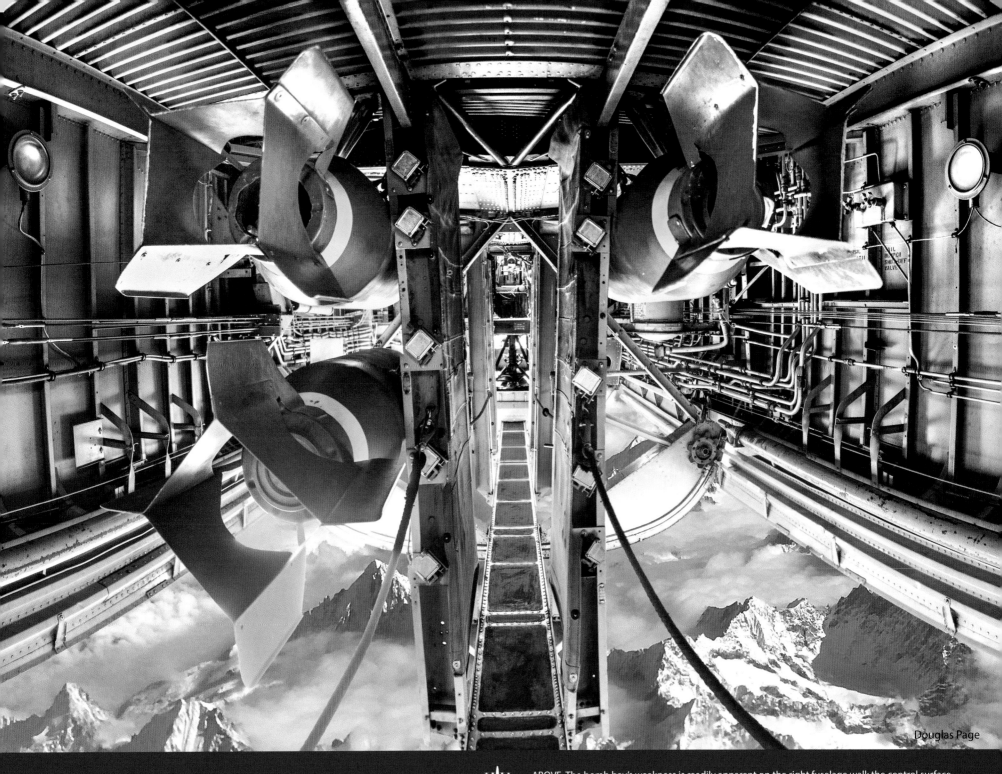

Douglas Page

ABOVE The bomb bay's weakness is readily apparent on the right fuselage wall: the control surface cables and hydraulic storage tanks and lines are protected by only a thin skin of aluminum.

POWERPLANT

IF THE LIBERATOR was the war's workhorse aircraft, then the Pratt & Whitney R-1830 was its equivalent in the engine realm. Invented in the 1930s as a more powerful version of the single-row, 800-hp "Wasp" engine, the "Twin Wasp" two-row, fourteen cylinder, air-cooled radial design displaced 1,830 cu in and produced 1,200 hp. Used in over thirty aircraft types, including the Douglas TBD Devastator, the Grumman F4F Wildcat, and the C-47 Skytrain, over 170,000 were produced by P&W as well as by automobile manufacturers Buick and Chevrolet. Many are still in use today, which is the single best reason *Witchcraft* still flies seventy years after the end of WWII.

The engine constantly improved, as seen by the numbers appended to the variants such as the R-1830-65, which had a top speed of 290 mph, a 28,000' ceiling, and a 2,100 mile range.

The engine, mount, cowling, and accessories are attached to the wing with just eight bolts, making engine removal relatively simple. In WWII, crews on tiny islands in the Pacific merely pulled a damaged engine and replaced it with another to keep the birds flying. The damaged engine was then sent to a refurbishment center where it was overhauled.

The engine's distinctive oval-shaped cowlings have side intakes that channel air to the oil cooler, the intercooler, and the turbo-supercharger. The engine nacelles are mounted nearly flush with the wing top to preserve the Davis wing's excellent laminar-flow aerodynamics.

Each engine has a 32 gallon oil tank. Because oil is less expensive than metal, the Twin Wasp was designed to burn and throw oil at the rate of about a gallon per hour.

Supercharger

The Twin Wasp includes a supercharger, an engine-driven compressor that increases the pressure of the air/fuel mixture provided to the carburetor, improving combustion. But with the increase in pressure also comes an increase of temperature, which is reduced by the engine's intercooler unit.

Turbo-supercharger

Later Twin Wasps featured a GE B-22 turbo-supercharger. (Nowadays it's simply called a turbocharger.) Located on the underside of the engine nacelle and looking eerily like a coiled serpent, the bladed turbine wheel, spun by exhaust gas, turns a shaft connected to a compressor, which pressurizes air that is then delivered to the carburetor, improving combustion and increasing manifold pressure. An adjustable waste gate controls the pressure of the exhaust gas passing by the turbine and thus its speed and the amount of compressed air that is generated.

Because the turbocharger does not automatically compensate for variations in turbine speed as the air density changes during climbs and descents, the pilots must adjust the four turbo control levers to maintain constant manifold pressure during such maneuvers.

The greatest advantage of the turbocharger is increased performance at higher altitudes, where the air is thinner and carburetor combustion less efficient. Its greatest disadvantage is the time needed for the turbo to "spool up" and deliver the power boost. This is because it takes time after closing the exhaust gate for the exhaust pressure to increase sufficiently to start spinning the turbine. "Twincharging," or using both the supercharger and the turbocharger in tandem, mitigates the weaknesses of both.

Propeller

Witchcraft's R-1830-65 engines use the Hamilton Standard hydromatic constant-speed prop. Engine speed is controlled by changes in propeller pitch. A governor on the engine adjusts the flow of oil inside the prop hub which compresses a piston that changes the propeller's "angle of attack," increasing or decreasing aircraft speed by taking bigger or smaller "bites" out of the air with the propeller blades.

When an engine is damaged, the propellers may continue spinning, often out of control, risking engine destruction and that of the aircraft as well. In such cases, "feathering," or changing the angle of attack so the edge of the propeller blade faces the wind, reduces this danger and is accomplished with an engine-mounted electric pump.

Electrical System

Two 24v batteries in the nose compartment output DC power, which is used to start the engines. Thereafter, the engines generate electricity for lighting, anti-icing pumps, bomb release, fuel boost and transfer pumps, the auxiliary hydraulic pump, engine instruments, radio and interphone, turrets, autopilot, propeller pitch governors and feathering pumps, cowl flaps, intercooler shutters, and warning lights. Inverters provide AC power to the turbo-supercharger regulators and the radio compass.

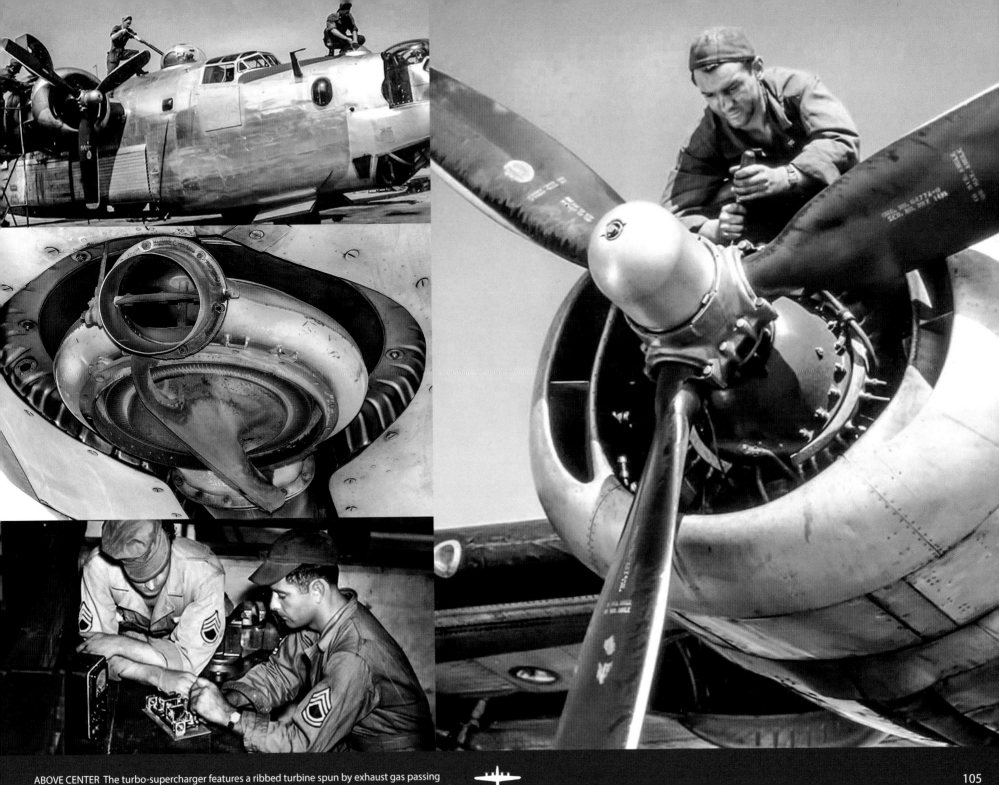

ABOVE CENTER The turbo-supercharger features a ribbed turbine spun by exhaust gas passing through the green manifold, controlled by the gate valve in the exhaust nozzle, presently opened.

LANDING GEAR

THOUGH BELOVED BY AFICIONADOS, tail-draggers are, for the most part, a thing of the past. Almost all modern aircraft use the tricycle gear of the sort pioneered by Reuben Fleet and Consolidated Aircraft due to its utility in beaching Consolidated float planes.

The Liberator's tall main gear consists of a 56" tire, with a rim joined to the strut with a single fork and a scissor joint to prevent torquing. Raised and lowered hydraulically, the main gear can also be manually positioned by turning a hand crank in the forward bomb bay which winds a cable that unlatches the up-lock, allowing the gear to drop into place under its own weight.

The mains retract outward, nesting into wells between the engines nacelles. Perhaps one of the most dazzling engineering feats in Liberator design is how the thin aluminum wing above the wells still manages to support an eighteen-ton aircraft (or almost twice that much when fully fueled and laden with bombs. And to think the engineers worked it out with a slide rule.

The tires themselves usually last about a hundred landings and can be retreaded. Tires this size are still available because they are used by one of the longest-lived aircraft ever built: the venerable Douglas DC-3, still in operation all over the world.

The original Liberator design called for a steerable nose wheel, but cost and weight, as well as widespread pilot familiarity with non-steerable tail wheels, meant the Liberator would feature a castering nose wheel with a single fork steel strut, two shimmy dampers, and a scissors joint to prevent undue twisting and wheel oscillation.

At first, nose wheel shimmy was such a problem that early Liberator crews carried a spare nose wheel with them when they went overseas. Improvement of the dampers and better training resolved the issue.

But when the first B-24Ds arrived in Australia in late 1942, they were plagued with a series of nose wheel failures that had crews rightfully alarmed. The problem was traced to the shearing off of the bolts fastening the actuating cylinder to the gear. Though the solution was simply to upgrade to a case-hardened bolt, many airmen continued to believe that the Liberator's nose gear was weak.

Their concerned seemed well-grounded when a number of C-87s (the cargo version of the B-24) flying over the Himalayas had nose wheel collapses. After investigation, it was determined that the nose wheel was not defective per se. Designed with a bomber in mind (which took off heavy and landed much lighter), the added weight of a transport on landing put great stress on the gear. The solution was simple but failed to satisfy pilots: Land on the mains and stay off the nose wheel as long as possible.

The nose wheel tilts backward into the nose and the outward-opening doors (necessitated by the nose redesign accompanying the installation of the Emerson nose turret) close behind it. The doors are designed to give way to provide an emergency exit and thus are painted red as a reminder to not put undue pressure on them. If the hydraulic system fails, a lever under the flight deck is thrown and the wheel shock strut is lifted to a point where the wheel drops and locks into position under its own weight.

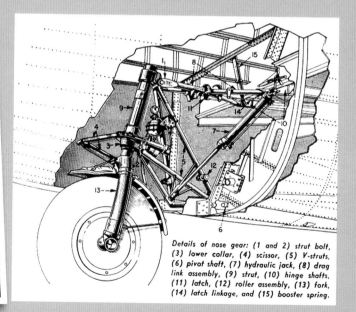

Details of nose gear: (1 and 2) strut bolt, (3) lower collar, (4) scissor, (5) V-struts, (6) pivot shaft, (7) hydraulic jack, (8) drag link assembly, (9) strut, (10) hinge shafts, (11) latch, (12) roller assembly, (13) fork, (14) latch linkage, and (15) booster spring.

ABOVE The crew of *Don't Cry Baby* (8/389/565) shed some bitter tears when, after bombing the Belfort, France, marshalling yards, the nose gear of their beloved B-24J collapsed on landing.

CONTROL SURFACES AND SYSTEMS

The Famous Split Tail

The defining visual characteristic of the B-24 is of course its split tail, which was developed for the flying boats that Consolidated built in the 1930s. For the Liberator, a couple of extra feet of width was added to the horizontal stabilizers to put the vertical fins directly behind the engines, which resulted in greater rudder authority. Though later wind-tunnel tests showed that a single vertical stabilizer performed better, the split tail served the Liberator well throughout its short but important lifespan and became a sort of trademark. The construction of the vertical fins is apparent from the photo: the oval curve is created by overlapping strips of aluminum.

Wings

Though its real world performance never quite lived up to the remarkable wind tunnel tests at CalTech, the high-aspect (length divided by chord, or width) Davis wing nevertheless lifted almost twice the payload of the B-17 Flying Fortress. And, though inherently unstable, the wings' roll stability was increased with a 3° dihedral, or upwards, tilt from root to tip. On the other hand, the horizontal stabilizers are flat in relation to each other.

Construction

The aircraft is constructed of just 5% steel, which is concentrated in the landing gear and engines. The other 95% is a stressed aluminum framework with a monocoque skin (an external structural system that supports loads, much the way an eggshell does) riveted together with sheets of Alclad, a trademarked high-strength aluminum, copper, manganese, and magnesium alloy. Though it is heavier than aluminum, it is also more corrosion-resistant.

Fly-by-Cable

All Liberator control surfaces are cable-actuated, except for the hydraulic metal flaps. Rudders, ailerons, and elevators are fabric covered, because they are cable-controlled and need to be as light as possible. When the pilot presses on the rudder pedal, a cable runs from his pedal to the control surfaces sixty feet behind him. These control cables are exposed on the interior of the fuselage. This results in a heavy, ponderous aircraft which someone once described as like "sitting on the front porch and flying a house."

The joke after the war was that a Liberator pilot could be picked out of a line-up because of his heavily-muscled left forearm, developed by horsing the yoke one-handed while he worked the engine throttles with the other.

Hydraulics

Notwithstanding all the cables, a visit to the bomb bay reveals a forest of hydraulic piping running along both fuselage walls, which operate the gear, flaps, bomb bay doors, brakes, autopilot, and the Consolidated A-6B nose turret. (Tail and ball turrets have their own, independent hydraulic systems.) These crucial hydraulic lines are shielded from enemy fire by just .0025 of an inch of aluminum skin, making them exceedingly vulnerable. As a result, many a Liberator had to land without hydraulics, the gear hand-cranked into place and the crew holding on for dear life with no brakes and a runway that was quickly being used up. But it could be done... and was.

Fowler Flaps

Maximizing the Davis wing's efficiency requires a good amount of speed; its performance at slow speeds is marginal. The metal Fowler Flaps, powered by hydraulic pressure activating a cable and pulley system, roll backwards on five steel tracks, lengthening the wing chord (width) and allowing the aircraft to fly at safely at lower speeds, useful in landing, take-off, and slow flight. Though a maximum flap setting of 40° degrees increases the wing area and lift by 55%, it also increases drag by a whopping 70%. A single hydraulic jack supplies power to actuate the flaps for both wings, a design weakness.

Fuel

The wings are made up of five sections stiffened by two massive spars: wing tips connect to outer sections that are bolted to an immense, thick center section, inside of which are located twelve interconnected fuel tanks. Three supplemental fuel tanks—called "Tokyo tanks" for the added range they confer—are outboard of both the #1 and #4 engines.*

At a burn rate of fifty gallons per hour per engine, the aircraft's 3,000 gallon fuel capacity (not including the 700 gallons that the two rubber bomb bay fuel tanks hold), yields up to fifteen hours airtime.

FLYING THE LIBERATOR

THERE IS LITTLE DISAGREEMENT: flying the Liberator is like "flying a half-full bathtub." The three flight axes: pitch (up/down), roll (wing up/down), and yaw (left/right), require constant pilot input. Any turbulence reverberates throughout the aircraft, like sitting on a long diving board with someone jumping up and down on the end.

The ailerons and rudders are nevertheless light compared to the elevator, which is heavy compared to the B-17, and full use of the ailerons is not uncommon in turbulence. Coordinated turns require rudder and aileron input and passenger movement about the aircraft requires constant trimming of control surfaces.

And as difficult as flying the aircraft is, taxiing is even harder. One of the first large aircraft with a nose wheel, the Liberator is widely known as one of the most difficult to taxi, resulting in an intricate dance using rudder, brakes, and differential engine power. The primary means of steering are the rudder pedal hydraulic toe brakes, which do nothing for the first two inches of travel as they accumulate pressure and then grab with a vengeance, locking tires, throwing everyone forward. A pilot has to literally be on his toes.

And yet it was flown by teenagers from all across America, many of whom had never been in an airplane prior to beginning their flight training. They mastered the incredibly complex, heavy aircraft, so what better authority on flying the B-24 than a young man?

Robert Pinksten is just 21 but has flown dozens of aircraft types in his short life, from trainer biplanes to the Me-262 jet. He finds the Liberator challenging. "You can set cruise at the same power settings and end up at different speeds," he says. "It's called being on or off the 'step.' At our preferred cruise speed of 165 mph, to get 'on' the step, we climb above the intended altitude and then descend to it. If you simply climb *to* the intended altitude, you'll find yourself in a nose-up attitude, slogging along at 145 mph. It's definitely not intuitive!"

"One of the hardest things to do in the B-24 is to taxi in a straight line," says Pinksten. "I use the brakes as little as possible. The wide separation of the engines creates asymmetrical thrust and if there's any wind you can get into trouble fast!"

Watching Pinksten taxi reminds one of a concert pianist. He "tickles" the four engine throttles constantly, increasing and decreasing each minutely in turn, focusing most of his attention on the inner engines which, due to their placement on the wing, generate airflow over the rudders, resulting in greater ground steering authority.

Though B-17 pilots brag about the flight characteristics of their preferred aircraft, the Liberator handles better in a crosswind. "I would take the B-24 into a 25-knot crosswind and never think twice," says Pinksten. "The B-17 in those same conditions would be a struggle and I personally wouldn't even try it. The difference is the Liberator's split tail, which has almost twice the rudder surface as the Fortress. In addition, there are two rudders and because the B-24 fuselage blocks the crosswind, the far rudder remains more effective. Finally, a nosewheel—even a castering nosewheel like the Liberator has—is inherently more directionally stable than the B-17's locking tailwheel."

But lest Liberator lovers get too puffed up, Pinksten reminds us that taxiing and crosswind landings form a very small part of flying the B-24. "It is always demanding," he says, "and it requires your attention 100% of the time, especially on the ground. The same reasons that make it an incredible plane to fly today made it unpopular among crews during the war."

He shakes his head. "It must have been something flying those ten hour missions with the rudimentary autopilots of the time—incredibly mentally and physically taxing, never mind being shot at by fighters. And if I work as hard as I do with the light turbulence we face during our daytime VFR flights, I can't imagine what flying through flak would be like."

But for Rob Pinksten, it's not just the challenge and fun of flying the aircraft. "When you sit in the cockpit and look across all those well-worn gauges, dials, and levers, you realize that you're sitting where history was made. It's humbling. The men and women of that period were truly the greatest generation and operating the aircraft today gives us a tiny but invaluable glimpse into what they did to defend our freedom. It's a privilege."

That's solid wisdom for any age.

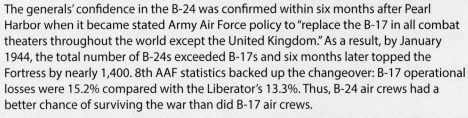

WORLD WAR II has been over for seventy years. The Axis powers have been turned into allies, their economies rebuilt due to American generosity via the Marshall Plan and a desire for peaceful reconciliation.

But one battle still rages. Whenever a B-17 aficionado meets a B-24 fan, a friendly skirmish breaks out and it isn't long before Fortress loyalists are lobbing verbal incendiary bombs, calling the Liberator a "flying boxcar," a "flying coffin," an "agony wagon," and the most painful—and funniest: the "box the B-17 came in."

B-24 defenders set their jaws and remark that flying a B-17 is like tootling around in a four-engine Piper Cub—it takes a *real* pilot to fly the B-24.

Usually, neither of them were in the war, so perhaps a better source would be those who were:

"The Fortress was an honest aircraft, easy to fly in formation, with a low landing speed, and no major vices," said one pilot.

Another pilot said, "The Liberator was a difficult plane to fly, but like many things, if you ever mastered it, you could take special pride in yourself—a good B-24 pilot was a good pilot."

Henry "Hap" Arnold, Commanding General of the Army Air Force, said, "The B-17 is a fine, heavy bomber which has been lavishly built up by the press... the B-24 has had remarkable success against German and Italian opposition [but] neither of those theaters has had the publicity enjoyed by the B-17 in the United Kingdom."

General George Kenney, commanding Allied Air Forces in the Southwest Pacific, was blunt: "The B-24 is the best thing we had until the B-29 was ready. It carried more bombs than the B-17. It could be flown while greatly overloaded, so it had much greater range. It was well-built and would take a surprising amount of punishment and still stay together. [But] it was not as nice a flying machine as the B-17. It never seemed ready to take off by itself, no matter how far you let it run. Its performance at high altitude was inferior but that made little difference to us in the Pacific. All things considered, our bomber crews were quite happy with the B-24. They didn't boast about its flying qualities but they appreciated its range and load-carrying capacity."

The generals' confidence in the B-24 was confirmed within six months after Pearl Harbor when it became stated Army Air Force policy to "replace the B-17 in all combat theaters throughout the world except the United Kingdom." As a result, by January 1944, the total number of B-24s exceeded B-17s and six months later topped the Fortress by nearly 1,400. 8th AAF statistics backed up the changeover: B-17 operational losses were 15.2% compared with the Liberator's 13.3%. Thus, B-24 air crews had a better chance of surviving the war than did B-17 air crews.

Also, between October 1944 and the end of the war (except December, which was a virtual tie), B-24 bombing accuracy was better than the B-17 by as much as 20%.

Edward Reilly, who flew Liberators for the 8th AAF, said, "B-17s were tough, reliable, sleek, and beautiful. But if you look at the facts, the B-24 was a better bomber. It could outrun the B-17 by at least twenty knots, carry a ton more bombs, and hit targets 400 miles deeper into enemy territory."

As the combatants glare at each other while they silently formulate the next barbed rejoinder, an old, weathered B-24 pilot steps forward, puts a gnarled hand on each of their shoulders, and says, "Human-like, the B-24 is rugged and yet sensitive, crude looking and yet beautiful, clumsy and yet clean-lined. She is at all times temperamental. No two B-24s are alike. For weeks she can be gay and healthy, the engines sing and zoom, then, without warning, she can become unruly, her instruments register wrong, her controls become sluggish, her engines spit oil. One plane can hungrily lap up gas, another sips it lady-like, another can tear away and fly faster than her sisters, while still another can only snail along. One plane is wing weighted, another is tail heavy. She has her moods. She needs attention; at times the attention of a squawking baby, at others she gaily bounces along, cat-purring with contentment."

Everyone smiles. Planes *are* like people, aren't they? Each one is unique, with its own strengths and weaknesses.

But the question persists: Is the B-24 a better plane than the B-17?

Perhaps not, but it is a better bomber, and that's why it was built.

THE SKY'S THE LIMIT

IN 1910, WHEN he was 23 and developing lumber tracts in Washington state, Reuben Fleet made $27,000. In 1941, as majority stockholder of Consolidated Aircraft, the fastest-growing company in America, he cleared less than $10,000 with investment income of $1.7 million. But Roosevelt's Tax Act, which would take effect 1 January 1942, was set to take 93% of that, and California 6%, leaving him with 1%: just $17,000.

So on 28 November 1941, Fleet sold his 1/3 interest and paid a 15% capital gains tax instead of the 25% that would soon become effective. "I unloaded at the right time," he said, "and didn't let the glamour of aviation get the better of my judgment."

Consolidated was acquired by the Aviation Corporation, which controlled Vultee Aircraft, a small builder of fighter and trainer airplanes in Los Angeles. Pearl Harbor occurred, production kicked into overdrive, and soon the company was being called "Convair." During the war it oversaw production in ten states, employed 100,000 people, and turned out 8.2% of all U.S. warplane production.

New models were developed during and after the war (see page 34) and in 1953, at the dawn of the jet age, Convair was purchased by General Dynamics Corporation, a conglomerate of military and high-tech companies. Convair continued as a division of General Dynamics, pioneering delta-winged aircraft like the F-102 Delta Dagger and the F-106 Delta Dart, culminating in its last bomber, the B-58 Hustler intercontinental nuclear bomber, which first flew in 1956. Capable of Mach 2 speeds, its sonic boom introduced the startled American public to supersonic flight.

In 1957, Convair's development of missile and rocket projects culminated in the Atlas rocket, which was first designed as an ICBM for the Air Force. When Martin Aircraft's Titan II eclipsed it, the Atlas transitioned into a civilian launch vehicle and put the Mercury astronauts into space. On 20 February 1962, an Atlas 6 rocket put astronaut John Glenn into orbit in *Friendship 7*. In the years since, the Atlas rocket has boosted over one hundred satellites into space and continues to be a time-tested launch vehicle.

In 1972, General Dynamics beat out Northrup and won the Air Force contract to build what has become the most successful jet fighter in history: the F-16 Fighting Falcon, 4,000 of which were built at the old Consolidated Fort Worth, TX, factory.

In 1994, General Dynamics split up and sold the Convair Division to former competitors McDonnell Douglas, Lockheed, and Martin Marietta. But in 1999, it returned to aviation, acquiring Gulfstream Aerospace.

In 2003, General Dynamics purchased the defense divisions of General Motors and is now a major supplier of armored vehicles of all types, including the M1 Abrams tank.

Though he died in 1975, it seems safe to assume that were he alive, Reuben Fleet would not be at all surprised by the impressive legacy of the little company he founded in 1923. His motto "Nothing short of right is right" remains the hallmark of not only his work, but of those who stand in his long shadow.

B-58 Hustler

F-17 Fighting Falcon

Gulfstream G650

M1 Abrams

COLLINGS FOUNDATION

This study in burgundy features a 1944 Grumman B-21 Goose, Al Capone's 1940 V-16 Cadillac, and a 1937 Cord Model 812.

THE MISSION

THE STATED PURPOSE of the Collings Foundation* is to organize and support living history events and exhibit artifacts that teach Americans about their heritage. Founded in 1977, the Foundation's original focus was transportation-related events such as antique car rallies, hill climbs, carriage and sleigh rides, and a winter ice-cutting festival in the Stow, MA, area. In the mid-1980s, these activities were broadened to include nationwide aviation-related events such as air shows, barnstorming demonstrations, historical reunions, and joint museum displays.

Since 1989, a major Foundation focus has been the "Wings of Freedom Tour" which now showcases the B-24 Liberator *Witchcraft,* the B-17 Flying Fortress *Nine-O-Nine,* the B-25 Mitchell *Tondelayo,* and the TF-51D Mustang *Toulouse Nuts.*

The Wings of Freedom Tour honors our veterans' sacrifices and educates visitors about America's involvement in WWII. For almost thirty years, the Tour has brought these historically important aircraft to over three million people per year, visiting over a hundred locations annually.

All across the country, volunteers support the Foundation's mission by hosting the aircraft tours at their local airport, hanging posters, and contacting media outlets. They also do gate duty, sell merchandize, enforce the safety zone surrounding the aircraft, and act as docents, teaching about the aircraft and their place in American history.

In addition to touring the interior of the aircraft, many visitors avail themselves of the opportunity to support the Foundation's goals and honor our veterans by taking a "flight experience," a thirty-minute flight aboard one of Foundation's touring aircraft.

To honor Vietnam veterans, the Foundation developed the "Vietnam Memorial Flight" featuring a McDonnell F-4D Phantom II, a Douglas TA-4J Skyhawk, a Bell UH-1E Huey, a F-100F Super Sabre, and a T-33 Shooting Star, all painted in the livery of notable aircraft of the era. The VMF attends air shows and living history events, offering rides and flight training.

The Foundation also sponsors restoration and maintenance workshops. As of 2017, restorations were underway on a F6F-3 Hellcat, an Fw 190F Würger (Shrike), a 1914 Curtiss Model F flying boat, a P-38 Lightning, a B-17G Flying Fortress, plus various military vehicles.

The Wings of Freedom Tour aircraft are annually maintained in New Smyrna Beach, FL. In Stow, MA, Foundation volunteers provide countless hours of enthusiastic and welcome labor in the restoration and maintenance of military vehicles and artifacts. In addition, they assist in the living history events.

Foundation headquarters include a museum celebrating historically significant aircraft and land vehicles, as well as vintage automobiles and race cars. The museum is open by appointment for group tours from May through October. It hosts fund-raising events for non-profit groups. There are three annual public living history events: Father's Day Weekend, The Race of the Century, and the popular WWII reenactment, The Battle for the Airfield.

Over the last three decades, the Foundation has undertaken and completed more restoration projects than many major U.S. aviation museums, including the Smithsonian National Air and Space Museum and the United States Air Force Museum. Foundation restorations have won the Grand Champion Warbird Award four times at America's premiere air show, EAA Air Venture at Oshkosh, WI.

Current and former commercial and military pilots and mechanics donate their time to fly and maintain these warbirds so passengers can experience first-hand the thrill of flying in an iconic, historic bomber or receive hands-on aerobatics instruction in the TF-51 Mustang *Toulouse Nuts.*

Volunteers return year after year for all these experiences, but most of all they enjoy meeting the veterans who flew these aircraft and preserved our freedom. Through the Foundation's efforts, as the WWII generation "goes west," their children, grandchildren, and many others are being reminded of their remarkable achievements.

* The Collings Foundation is a nonprofit corporation organized under the laws of the state of Massachusetts.

1913 Stutz Bearcat

1931 Studebaker President Sedan

1930 Cord Model L29 Coupe

1927 Rolls Royce Springfield Phantom 1 Phaeton

Michael Andretti Lola/Ford XB Indycar

1935 Packard Model 1208 Sedan

1932 Deusenberg SJ Phaeton

All images Glenn Perry / www.gperryimages.com

* And many more, including a 1906 Stanley Steamer Touring Car, 1916 Chevrolet Baby Grand touring car, 1924 Ford Model T, 1928 Packard Phaeton, 1937 Rutherford sprint car, and a 1996 R&S MkIII/Ford.

AIRCRAFT COLLECTION*

Vought F4U-5NL Corsair

Bell UH-1E Iroquois

Boeing PT-17 Stearman Kaydet

Messerschmitt Me-262 Schwalbe

Grumman TBM Avenger

North American F-100F Super Sabre

McDonnell-Douglas F-4D Phantom II

McDonnell TA-4J Skyhawk

North American B-25 Mitchell

* And many more, including a 1909 Bleriot XI monoplane, 1942 Cessna UC-78 Bobcat, 1942 Fieseler Fi-156C-1 Storch, Grumman S-2F Tracker, Douglas A1-E Skyraider, and Grumman FM-2 Wildcat.

Supermarine Spitfire Mk. IX

John Dibbs

Biggin Hill Heritage in England recently completed the restoration of this extremely rare combat veteran of 116 missions over Europe, flown by two combat aces.

Grumman F6F-3N Hellcat

During the war, this Hellcat was part of VF(N)-76, the highest scoring night fighter squadron in the U.S. Navy. Now, it's being painstakingly restored to its full glory.

North American TF-51D Mustang

The newest addition to the Foundation's fighter collection, *Toulouse Nuts* received the Grand Champion restoration prize at Air Venture 2016 in Oshkosh, WI.

Curtiss P-40B Tomahawk

John Dibbs

Salvaged from a later crash, this airplane is the world's only P-40B and only airworthy American fighter to survive the Japanese attack on Pearl Harbor 7 December 1941.

PRESERVING OUR PAST...

All photos David Watts, Jr.
His book, *Battle for the Airfield,* is available at www.dwattsjr.com.

The "Battle for the Airfield" is an event that takes place every October dramatizing a fictional Allied attack on a German-held airstrip, It features scores of re-enactors and period vehicles.

WORKING HARD...

...AND DOING SO PROUDLY.

COLLINGS FOUNDATION · 137 Barton Road · P.O. Box 248 · Stow, MA 01775

JOIN US!

YOU

AFTERWORD

WORLD WAR ONE ended with the Allies' boot planted firmly on Germany's neck, pressing its face into the mud. At least that's how the Germans saw it. Humiliated yet resolute, they waited for their time to come again.

Thus, Hitler's rise to power was predictable. Destroy the pride of a proud people and they will fight to regain it. As Germany secretly rearmed in the 1930s, the west became mired in a recession that, through government incompetence, widened and deepened into a global depression, further stoking the fires of isolationism and fear.

Coincident was the rise of socialism and militarism in Russia and Japan respectively. Like all totalitarian regimes, they waited for the opposition of free peoples and when none came, the Tsar was killed in Russia and the Samurai took control in Japan.

But some prescient souls in the west were paying attention and pushed for rearmament for the coming, inevitable war. Reuben Fleet was one of these, an energetic entrepreneur whose fledgling company started out producing others' designs, then developed its own, preparing for the day when the Army Air Force would realize it needed a long-range, heavy-payload bomber only it could build.

Flown for the first time just weeks after the outbreak of World War II, the B-24 Liberator went from concept to prototype in an unprecedented nine short months. Its design weaknesses were overlooked in favor of its strengths, a 3,000-mile range and an 8,000-pound payload. It was tailor-made for the first truly worldwide war.

And it served remarkably well in every theater of that war, hauling fuel over the Himalayas to our Chinese nationalist allies, skimming jungle tops in the South Pacific dropping supplies to troops, softening up distant islands before dozens of amphibious assaults, rising amid swirling sands in North Africa to harass Erwin Rommel, roaring across the Danube Basin at fifty feet to bomb the Ploiesti refineries, showing the Brits that daylight formation strategic bombing was indeed possible, countering the Nazi U-boat threat to North Atlantic shipping and thus saving Britain from starvation, protecting America from bases on the frozen isles of the Bering Sea, and ranging across the Indian Ocean as the RAF's favorite heavy bomber—in almost all these locales, the B-24 did what no other aircraft could have done.

Its replacement, the B-29 Superfortress, arrived the last year of the war and ushered in the atomic age, but the Liberator had already done the lion's share of the work.

The B-17 was prettier, flew nicer, was more comfortable, and was safer. But half again as many Liberators were built as the Flying Fortress, proof that it was a better bomber.

But the B-29 was better than both of them, and within five years the Liberator was summarily relegated to the scrap heap, smelted down to be reborn as pots, pans, and storm shutters all across America. Rarely in history has such an important weapon been so quickly forgotten. If not for the B-24s flown by the Indian Air Force after the war, we'd have nothing but pictures to remember its remarkable legacy by.

But another generation of prescient people recognized that the past is prologue and forgetting what went before is tantamount to ordering up previous mistakes anew. At great cost of time and money, the Collings Foundation restored an aircraft that now stands as a lone representative of the over 18,000 Liberator bomber variants that were built between 1940 and 1945. And it is highly unlikely that another bomber airframe will be returned to flying status as *Witchcraft* has been.

Hence this book, an effort to remind us all of the fortuitous existence of this mighty plane which burst from the minds of geniuses, served gallantly to help win a war, and was then unceremoniously discarded as outdated.

I hope the preceding corrects that in a small way. My father flew the Liberator, so I am inclined to respect the aircraft for that reason alone. But when my studies took me into the far-flung theaters of WWII, I found the Liberator everywhere, supplying troops, saving lives, and pummeling enemies. So far-reaching were its missions and so impressive its accomplishments that I dare say I would have become an admirer even if I wasn't required to be one by the plain and simple fact that this ugly, unpressurized, uninsulated, and reportedly unsafe aircraft saved my father's life more than once.

A sincere thank you to everyone who helped make this book a reality (some of whom don't even know it): Dave Barnett, Allen Benzing, Jack Berger, Larry Carner, Hunter Chaney, Bob Collings, Rich Davidson, Gary Dunn, Cheri Gittins, Jim Goolsby, Mark Henley, Tom Jeffrey, Ryan Keogh, Gary Lichty, Mac McCauley, Dave Matheny, Jamie Mitchell, Douglas Page, Robert Pinksten, John Purdy, Paul Reidy, Justin Slagowski, Greg Trebon, Steve Weigandt, Elaine Martin-Weigandt, and Robert Wyatt, the many dedicated volunteers of the Wings of Freedom Tour, and, most importantly, the veterans who inspired me to do it.

Witchcraft flew 137 missions during World War II, thousands of hours for the IAF thereafter, and has now completed almost thirty years of nationwide touring that surely places this airframe at the head of an elephantine procession leading toward victory, freedom, and peace.

Elephantine? Perhaps "majestic" is more apt.

– Kenny Kemp

SOURCES

Birdsall, Steve. *The B-24 Liberator*. New York: Arco Publishing Company, Inc., 1968.

_____. *Log of the Liberators*. New York: Doubleday & Company, Inc., 1973.

Blue, Allan G. *The B-24 Liberator*. New York: Charles Scribner's Sons, 1976.

Bowman, Martin. *B-24 Combat Missions*. New York: Metro Books, 2009.

Davis, Larry. *B-24 Liberator in Action*. Carrollton, TX: Squadron/Signal Publications, 1987.

Dorr, Robert. *B-24 Liberator Units of the Pacific War*. Oxford, U.K: Osprey Publishing, 1999.

Douglas, Graeme. *Consolidated B-24 Liberator Owner's Workshop Manual*. Somerset, U.K: Haynes Publishing, 2013.

Doyle, David. *B-24 Liberator in Action*. Carrollton, TX: Squadron/Signal Publications, 2012.

Johnson, Paul. *Modern Times*. New York: Harper & Row, Publishers, 1983.

Kinzey, Bert. *B-24 Liberator in Detail*. Carrollton, TX: Squadron/Signal Publications, 2000.

Liberator. Fort Worth, TX: General Dynamics Convair Division, 1989.

Wagner, William. *Reuben Fleet*. Fallbrook, CA: Aero Publishers, Inc., 1976.

Watts, Perry. *The Famous B-24 Witchcraft*. Atglen, PA: Schiffer Publishing, Ltd., 2015.

Welsh, Ralph. *Wow!* San Francisco, CA: Welsh Printing, 2013.

Rich Davidson

ET CETERA

ALSO BY KENNY KEMP

Fedora / Wildest Dreams (DVD)
I Hated Heaven
Dad Was a Carpenter
The Welcoming Door
The Carpenter of Galilee
City on a Hill
Oki's Island
Lightland
Parables for Today
The Wise Man Returns
Flying with the Flak Pak

AVAILABLE AT

kennykemp.com
flyingwiththeflakpak.com
facebook.com/kenny.kemp
witchcraftb24.com
amazon.com

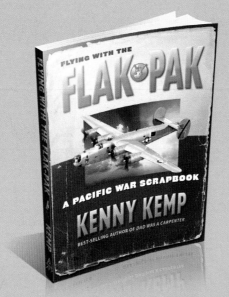

FLYING WITH THE FLAK PAK
A Pacific War Scrapbook

Follow a young B-24 Liberator pilot through his training and deployment in the Pacific Theater.

Softcover, full-color, 266 pages, 1,000 illustrations

World War II is brought vividly to life in this well-crafted labor of love and appreciation. – Booklist

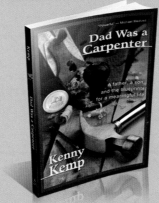

DAD WAS A CARPENTER
A father, a son, and the blueprints for a meaningful life

This Grand Prize winner of the National Self-Published Book Award is a moving companion piece to *Flak Pak*.

Softcover, 110 pages

An astoundingly touching memoir. – Publishers Weekly